THE SCIENCE OF READING IN PRACTICE

JULIA B. LINDSEY

SMALL GROUPS, BIG RESULTS

Evidence-Based Routines to Get Every Child Reading

SCHOLASTIC

To teachers who do all they can for their readers,
who've stayed up late to prepare a lesson,
who've needed that extra cup of coffee.
I see you, and I thank you for all you do.

Senior Vice President and Publisher: Tara Welty
Executive Editorial Director: Sarah Longhi
Editor-in-Chief: Raymond Coutu
Production Editor: Danny Miller
Assistant Editor: Samantha Unger
Cover design: Tannaz Fassihi
Interior design: Maria Lilja

Classroom photos courtesy of Abigail Gaddis of Abigail K Photography and educators Nadia Boria, Kari Tunstill, and Elaine Shobert. All other photos © Shutterstock.com.

Credits: 17: "The Active View of Reading" from "The Science of Reading Progresses: Communicating Advances Beyond the Simple View of Reading" by Nell K. Duke and Kelly B. Cartwright. Originally published in *Reading Research Quarterly*, Volume 56. Copyright © 2021 by the Authors. Reprinted by permission of John Wiley & Sons, Inc.; 34: "Multidimensional Fluency Scale" from *The Megabook of Fluency* by Timothy V. Rasinski and Melissa Cheesman Smith. Copyright © 2025, 2018 by Timothy V. Rasinski and Melissa Cheesman Smith. Used by permission of Timonthy V. Rasinski and Melissa Cheesman Smith; 83: "What Is a Kiwi?" from Readworks.org by Peggy Lindsey. Used by permission of Readworks.org; 97: Pages from *Nic Bishop Big Cats* © 2019 by Nic Bishop and *Phonics First Little Readers: Shhh!* by John Shefelbine © Scholastic Inc. Used by permission of Scholastic Inc. All rights reserved.

ISBN 978-1-5461-5047-3

2 3 4 5 6 7 8 9 10 40 34 33 32 31 30 29 28 27 26

Scholastic Inc., 557 Broadway, New York, NY 10012

Contents

Acknowledgments

This book stands on the legacy, knowledge, and friendship of so many incredible individuals, listed here and beyond.

Thank you, first and foremost, to the amazing Scholastic Professional Books team. To Ray and Sarah, you have my utmost respect and gratitude for all you've done to ensure this book exists and can support teachers. To the entire Scholastic team, thank you for all your careful work helping me create a beautiful book.

Thank you to my wonderful husband, Raub. We'll put this book in the "believe in yourself" category. What a year we've had, but in all its messiness, my constant source of support, love, and happiness is always you. To Kiwi, our dog, thank you for staying with us for a bit longer. Many thanks to my family and friends who've heard way too much about reading instruction over the years.

To my reading friends, thank you for engaging in years and years of conversation, debate, reading, rereading, and edits. This book wouldn't exist without you.

In particular, Elaine Shobert, Kate Franz, Linda Rhyne, Neena Saha, Lori Sappington, Nadia Boria, Jaime Clarke, Kari Tunstill, Laura Veihl, Jennifer Nelson, and Beka Johnson, for all your comments, thank you!

To the schools and teachers who have already worked with me to transform small-group instruction, thank you for trusting me and for sharing your stories. I am so proud to be a part of the wonderful work you do on behalf of children.

To the researchers, experts, and educators whose work shaped this book, thank you. Your work makes a difference.

Foreword
by Matthew Burns

Reading instruction in the country is changing. Some might herald the recent changes as revolutionary, while some might say that they are too little, too late. I fall into the former category. I have been involved in education for over 25 years, and in that time, I have never seen changes like we are seeing today. Teachers are embracing scientific findings and their implications for instruction. They are using data to more precisely address students' needs. And they are closely monitoring the results using evidence-based assessment tools. Unfortunately, those exciting changes have also led to unintended consequences such as teachers having to rethink and retool their instruction on the fly.

There is likely no more controversial or more misunderstood aspect of teaching reading than small-group instruction. Over 25 years ago, the National Reading Panel (2000) found that small-group instruction was at least as effective as individual tutoring and whole-class instruction, and in some instances was even more effective. Armed with that information, teachers set out to teach small groups but had little guidance on how to do it well and, therefore, turned to old ideas and experiences. They determined supposed instructional levels using various informal reading inventories that had long been discredited (Nilsson, 2008; Pikulski, 1974; Spector, 2005) and grouped students with resulting data that was about as accurate flipping a coin (Parker et al., 2015). Needless to say, it did not go well; students did not learn, and teachers grew frustrated.

Today we know that small-group instruction is important for many reasons, perhaps the most important being that it provides an opportunity to differentiate instruction based on students' needs. Using data to identify students' strengths and challenges, and then using that information to target their needs through small-group instruction, consistently leads to positive effects (Hall & Burns, 2018), and, again, we see outcomes that are at least as positive, if not better, than one-on-one instruction (Begeny et al., 2018).

It seems that we examine reading skills using one of two extremes: with one global (and inaccurate) piece of information such as the student's instructional level, or with excessively detailed data attempting to cover every aspect of the student's reading development. As mentioned, using informal reading inventories to determine a supposed instructional level is not good practice, yet dissecting reading to a granular level for core instruction isn't either.

To differentiate small-group reading instruction, teachers simply need an understanding of generally how well students can use phonemic awareness to blend and segment sounds, how well they can break the code when reading, the extent to which they read with fluency, and the degree to which they understand what they read. That's it! As Dr. Lindsey points out in this book, that breakdown of student skill provides a starting point for small-group instruction, and most questions about students' needs can be addressed with data that is easy to obtain.

Although recent research has given us a much better understanding of small-group reading instruction, most practicing teachers have not been trained in how to use it to create small groups and deliver instruction, and are, as a result, once again building airplanes as they are flying them.

Small Groups, Big Results provides answers to questions that you are likely asking. It describes how to use data to group students based on strengths and needs, how to organize and schedule small groups, and how to make them go more smoothly. It contains 21 detailed routines to address target needs—from developing phonemic awareness to comprehending complex texts. *Small Groups, Big Results* is a remarkably practical, easy-to-use book, based on scientific research. Upon reading it, you will be able to put Dr. Lindsey's ideas into practice the very next day. It is clear she is a former classroom teacher.

Small-group instruction can unlock students' potential, and *Small Groups, Big Results* will help you solve the mystery about how to implement it. I am confident that it will help you continue to change reading instruction and be widely used. I look forward to seeing the results.

Matthew Burns
Rose and Irving Fien Professor of Special Education and Assistant Director of the University of Florida Literacy Institute (UFLI) at the University of Florida

Introduction

Dear Reader,

I have a confession to make: When I was in the classroom, I hated teaching reading in small groups. Of everything I taught, there was nothing I disliked more than that hour each day. My school required a leveled benchmark/guided reading approach. You might be thinking, "Oh, okay. She probably hated it because that approach isn't ideal for developing decoding skills. She even wrote about that in *Reading Above the Fray*, her first book."

Nope. My disdain stemmed from the fact that I had no idea how to do small groups without spending hours and hours planning for it after school. So, my instruction ended up being really, well, variable. Some days, I copiously planned lessons, carefully selected resources, and focused on clear goals for my readers. Other days, I ended up grabbing a book at each group's instructional level and simply hoped for the best. I couldn't find a rhythm that allowed me to craft differentiated small-group instruction without giving up so much of my free time.

Looking back on my years in the classroom, I realize that planning time wasn't my only issue. Even when I did carefully plan, my instruction was not typically based on reliable assessment results, evidence-based practices, or anything else I was teaching at other points in the day. I was "doing small groups," but was I really teaching? I certainly wasn't targeting specific skills that research shows can help readers grow.

In the past several years, I've supported educators across the globe in learning about and implementing research-supported practices in literacy. Many different questions arise as educators shift their teaching, but one is common and near constant. From coaches in Michigan to teachers at international schools in Singapore to administrators in Kansas, everyone wants to know, "But what are we supposed to do about small-group reading?" which is often followed by this question: "What does the science of reading say about small-group reading?" Those educators, like me, know something needs to change.

And for good reason. Small-group literacy instruction has been the subject of quite a bit of controversy lately. In the United States, media coverage about three-cueing and guided reading has to date led 40 states and the District of Columbia to pass laws requiring science-backed reading instruction, many of which ban three-cueing. Some education advocates and journalists argue teachers should stop using small-group instruction because it leaves the majority of students to their own devices, likely wasting valuable teaching time. But all the while, teachers are left asking, "But what am I supposed to do when I have three fourth graders who still can't decode words and my school doesn't have any more intervention slots?"

How This Book Came to Be

Much as I did when I wrote *Reading Above the Fray*, I felt compelled to write this book because there is so much conversation about what not to do and very little about what to do.

Throughout the book, I propose one way to think about small-group instruction, which is based on available research and rooted in understandings of how reading develops. It is strongly influenced by my experience teaching and supporting teaching, and acknowledges the real constraints of actual schools and needs of actual children.

But it isn't the only reasonable way to think about small-group instruction. This idea, that maybe there isn't just one perfect, evidence-aligned way to talk about small-group instruction, held me back from writing this book for a long time.

As such, I struggled with the book's title. I considered *A Potential, Maybe Helpful Book With Some Solutions for Small-Group Instruction* to insinuate that my idea for rethinking small groups is just one of many reasonable ideas. I even considered avoiding the term "small group" altogether (too much baggage!). So, before you start reading, there are four important things I want you to know about this book.

1. None of the teaching routines, techniques, lessons, or ideas are specific to "small group." If the term "small group" makes you think about students spending an hour rotating between centers and leading reading groups, get ready to think again.

2. Talking about research related to small-group instruction is complicated. Among other issues, one prominent problem is that there is no consistent definition of small-group instruction other than a general agreement that it includes fewer students than all the students in a classroom. Thus, this book draws on research from a number of arenas to offer ideas for supporting students' needs.

3. I focus on small-group instruction in the general education classroom. Though it may offer some good ideas or insights for intervention or more specialized instruction, this book is primarily for classroom teachers who want to use small-group instruction, no matter what support exists outside their classroom.

4. The book assumes some knowledge of decoding, fluency, and comprehension, and how they develop. If you are looking for more information about those topics or more about core, whole-class instruction, I recommend resources throughout the book.

What About MTSS?

MTSS (Multi-Tiered Systems of Support) can be an incredibly powerful structure for supporting students' needs and organizing small-group instruction. However, it is a whole-school approach. In this book, I wanted to focus on small-group instruction that any teacher could use. As a teacher, I was frustrated by the number of challenges my students encountered in reading that I couldn't fix with the resources around me. Though some did require support outside my classroom, with the right routines, I could've solved some of these challenges in my classroom. I hope that this book provides you with some solutions so that, no matter how much help you have or what structures your school has, you can meet the needs of your readers.

How This Book Is Organized

Small Groups, Big Results is organized in two parts: "big picture" chapters and targeted routine chapters. You might not want to read it straight through because so much of it is about specific instructional routines. In essence, it is a hybrid professional book and resource, so you might read about a routine right when you need it.

Chapters 1, 2, and 3 set up the conversation with information and common questions about small-group reading instruction. I discuss what the research says, how to plan and organize for instruction, and how to assess students to determine their needs. I recommend reading these chapters and setting aside some time to discuss with colleagues how ideas in them fit into your classroom and school day. Some of the ideas may take some time to implement and some may not be possible in every context.

Chapters 4 through 8 introduce instructional routines that focus on what small-group instruction is best for: targeted instruction, practice, and application of specific skills with immediate, direct feedback. Each is deeply grounded in research. You'll immediately notice that four of the chapters focus on decoding and fluency, while only one focuses on comprehension. That's because the research supporting decoding instruction in small groups is clearer than the research supporting comprehension instruction in small groups.

I focus on skills and knowledge that research demonstrates (1) can be impacted significantly by targeted instruction; (2) are related to long-term growth in reading comprehension; and (3) can be efficiently and effectively supported in small-group instruction. Each chapter focuses on specific routines to solve common problems by intensifying instruction and ensuring students receive high-impact, feedback-driven practice.

What About Swaps?

If you've read *Reading Above the Fray*, you know I love instructional swaps! Swaps are a way of making change by embracing a new, effective practice and letting go of a familiar, less effective practice. Doing swaps doesn't mean adding more to the day. This book recommends eight big swaps that help us shift how we think about small-group instruction and replace problematic practices with more efficient, research-based ones. Look for them at the end of each chapter.

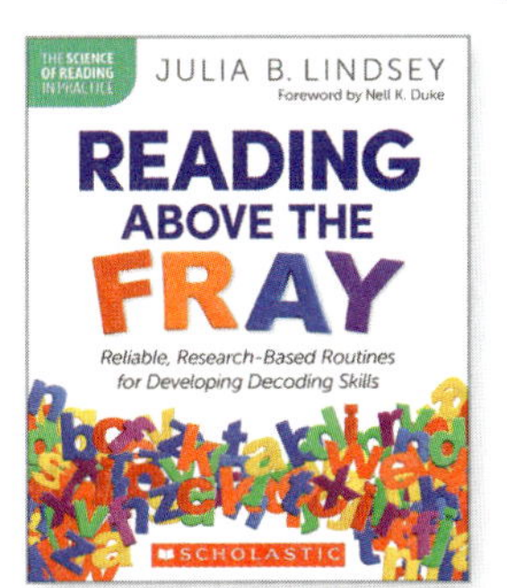

How to Use This Book

Whether you're a classroom teacher, interventionist, special educator, or administrator, there is something in *Small Groups, Big Results* for you.

Classroom teachers: Use Chapters 1–3 to figure out how you can best use small-group instruction in your classroom. After collecting student data, identify the categories students' skills fall into (see Chapter 2). Then focus your attention on the chapters that address those categories. If you're new to small-group instruction, start with just one routine.

Interventionists, special educators, and other specialists: You might not find Chapters 1–3 as useful as classroom teachers; however, the instruction routines in Chapters 4–8 may be helpful. Many are based on intervention research and can be integrated into your systematic, explicit support for students with specific reading needs.

Administrators: Start with Chapter 1 and Chapter 3's "Big Question" 10: How can an administrator support small-group instruction? Consider how small-group instruction is used in your school and what swaps (at the end of each chapter) might be most beneficial to your school before diving in further.

This book may not cover everything you need to know about small-group instruction. But I hope it empowers you to leverage small-group instruction as a powerful tool to purposefully support your readers. I hope this book leads to "aha" moments about the value of using small-group instruction in a targeted, purposeful way—moments that the educators I've worked with have had. I hope it helps your readers thrive and grow, becoming readers who can choose to read for whatever reasons they have, whether that be necessity, interest, or, yes, indeed, the simple pleasure of opening up a new book.

Happy teaching,

Julia

Small Groups, Big Ideas

CHAPTER 1

"By third grade, the range of reading abilities in a classroom can span 9.2 grade levels."

—Janine M. Firmender, Sally M. Reis, and Sheelah M. Sweeny (2013)

Put plainly: A third grader learning the alphabet may be sitting next to a classmate who's reading *Harry Potter and the Sorcerer's Stone*. Anyone who's been in a classroom knows that there is incredible variety in children's reading. Yet we, as educators, are expected to support them all and ensure they become proficient readers.

The clearest argument for differentiation is this: In most classrooms, students' needs are far more varied than a single experience, curriculum, or lesson can address. It borders on irrational to suggest a single teacher can meet that range of needs by delivering the same content to an entire class. About two-thirds of elementary school teachers report using small groups at least a few times a week to teach literacy, aiming to meet specific needs of their students (Lenski et al., 2016). Practically speaking, it just makes sense. Small groups allow for targeted instruction to meet diverse needs.

Small-group instruction can be purposeful and highly effective. Decades of research shows that when implemented well, it can build on effective whole-class instruction and accelerate reading achievement (Puzio et al., 2020; Slavin, 1993; Slavin et al., 2011). Studies also find that quality small-group instruction strengthens engagement and positive attitudes toward reading (Connor & Morrison, 2016; Kulik & Kulik, 1992; Lou et al., 1996).

The Argument for Small-Group Instruction

It may seem like a "no-brainer" to prioritize small-group instruction for the differentiation necessary to meet all students' needs. And yet, small-group instruction is a source of endless controversy and debate. To some, it is seen as a burden, a waste of time, or a routine that should only be carried out within a strict MTSS system. To others, small-group instruction is the most essential time of day for teaching readers. Why such strong, conflicting views?

First, small-group instruction is associated with several controversial, ineffective practices. According to a 2020 survey conducted by *EdWeek*, the most common type of small-group instruction was guided reading (Kurtz et al., 2020). Unfortunately, guided reading and its associated practices (using leveled texts, administering leveled benchmark assessments) are not aligned with or supported by research. While we can't afford to spend time on ineffective practices, the real danger is assuming all small-group instruction is fundamentally flawed.

Leaving Levels

A leveled approach focuses on reading development as a ladder of reading levels. If students can just climb up to the right level in each grade, as the approach seems to suggest, they will be successful readers. The approach also provides what feels like a clear, usable framework to plan for and deliver differentiated instruction: If a group of students can read and answer basic questions in a Level C text, teach a small group with Level D texts.

However, assigning reading levels to students does not give us specific insights into their skills in word recognition or comprehension (Hiebert, 2017). Research tells us that students do not always show consistent abilities when reading texts at the same level (Burns et al., 2015). That means just because a student reads one Level F text with 90 percent accuracy, it doesn't mean she will read another Level F text with the same accuracy, calling into question one of the major claims of leveled systems. That is likely because neither orthographic patterns in words, nor the content of texts, including vocabulary, topics, and text features, are introduced systematically (Burns et al., 2015; Pitcher & Fang, 2007).

Furthermore, research shows that a running record, the standard assessment in leveled systems, is not sensitive or specific enough to operate as a screener, meaning it cannot reliably tell us who is at risk or may need additional support (Klingbeil et al., 2017). Benchmark leveled text assessments are not reliable enough for decision-making, nor do they give us clear insight into students' skill or knowledge. They also take an enormous amount of time to administer (in my experience, that often comes out to 30 days over a year).

Leaving Levels *continued*

But what about the instruction we typically deliver during guided reading? Guiding students through texts might feel like we're helping them to become independent readers. Unfortunately, common guided reading practices are not aligned with current research and may even be hampering aspects of students' reading development (Burns et al., 2015). In a recent meta-analysis on differentiated literacy instruction, Kelly Puzio and his colleagues (2020) claim, "We could not find a single study on guided reading that employed an experimental or quasi-experimental design." In other words, there are no high-quality studies that give me confidence to recommend using guided reading to support readers.

One common guided reading strategy that has gotten substantial attention in the last few years is the three-cueing system, which is based on a debunked theory that good readers recognize unknown words based on a combination of information about meaning, syntax, and letters. In reality, good readers do not rely on multiple sources of information to recognize words (Ehri, 2014). They rely on decoding, or leveraging the connections between letters and sounds, even when reading words with rare sound-spelling connections (Castles et al., 2018). The most effective "system" for developing readers is to support them in their efforts to decode words (Rodgers et al., 2016). And my argument is not limited to decoding development. At present, there are also no high-quality studies showing that guided reading strengthens comprehension.

All that said, not everything about guided reading is bad. Many texts that are "leveled" can be great texts. For example, *Charlotte's Web* by E. B. White (which predates the Fountas & Pinnell leveling system by 40 years) is considered a Level R. In other words, some of the texts themselves are not a problem, but rather the overarching structure and rigidity of guided reading is not worth the time and effort.

Throughout this book, I offer you clear alternatives for understanding your readers (Chapter 2) and selecting texts (Chapter 3 and Chapters 4–8 in the step-by-step routines). I can't promise you that my suggestions will feel as easy to implement as the familiar, but problematic, practice of matching a student to a book at her "just right" level. But I can promise that they are based on current research, which, I hope, will give you the inspiration and confidence you need to move forward with your students.

Second, everyone uses the term "small group," but there is no universal definition. "Small group" is actually just a descriptor of group size, not of content or structure. That means it can look wildly different from classroom to classroom. Without a universal definition, it is not clear who small-group reading instruction is for, why it's done, or what purpose it serves.

Third, you might also be wondering about practical matters. Teachers and administrators frequently ask me questions such as, "What's the best way to form groups? How many days a week and how much time should I spend with each group? What's the best use of time for students I'm not working with?" Those are fair questions, but, the truth is, we do not always have strong research to answer some of our most pressing practical questions. That's part of the challenge! Because small-group instruction is not standardized, it's difficult to have clear, productive conversations about it.

Now the good news: Even though research doesn't yet provide all the answers, the answers it does provide can help us to make thoughtful, purposeful decisions about how, when, and why we carry out small-group instruction. In this chapter, I'll focus on the why by defining small-group instruction based on its purposes.

The Purposes of Small-Group Instruction

We'll start with the broadest definition. Small-group reading instruction could simply be what it sounds like: meeting with a few students from the class to teach them how to read. And that begs a question: What does a smaller group of students allow us to do that we cannot easily do with a larger group?

Smaller groups make it easier to target specific needs.

After identifying students' needs with data derived from assessments, we can use small-group instruction to provide targeted instruction, practice, and support. A recent meta-analysis found that the most effective small-group interventions target a specific skill (Hall & Burns, 2018). Instead of covering many areas of reading at once, we can focus deeply and effectively on just one or two. One helpful model for visualizing elements of proficiency is the Active View of Reading (Duke & Cartwright, 2021). Instruction targeting elements described in the Active View of Reading improves reading comprehension for both typically developing and struggling readers (Burns et al., 2023).

The Active View of Reading

(Duke & Cartwright, 2021)

Smaller groups make it easier to differentiate instruction.

Differentiated instruction—changing the content, task, or support to meet specific student needs—is more effective than one-size-fits-all instruction across word recognition, fluency, vocabulary, comprehension, and even writing (Connor et al., 2014; Begeny et al., 2018; Puzio et al., 2020; Reis et al., 2011; Wanzek et al., 2018). It benefits:

- multilingual learners (Baker et al., 2016; Dussling, 2020; Gersten et al., 2007; Hall et al., 2020)
- students with specific challenges (Hall & Burns, 2018)
- students with diagnosed learning differences, such as dyslexia (Al Otaiba et al., 2023)
- gifted students (Steenbergen-Hu et al., 2016)
- and many others (Baye et al., 2019; Faggella-Luby & Wardwell, 2011; Hatcher et al., 2005; Kamps et al., 2008; Nielsen & Friesen, 2012)

Smaller groups make it easier to ensure students get enough practice.

Children need an enormous amount of repetitive, engaging practice to master skills necessary for proficient reading. To build alphabet knowledge, for example, research-tested instruction often includes 60 or more chances for students to connect letter forms to sounds (Fitzgerald et al., 2020; Roberts, 2021). To build decoding skills, one study found that students benefit most from phonics lessons that include at least 1.8 practice opportunities per minute (Fien et al., 2015). In vocabulary, studies suggest that readers need about 12 repetitions reading and understanding a word to commit its meaning and spelling to memory (Nation, 2014).

Yes, students can get practice in larger group settings. But there are two challenges to that: Not all students are paying attention and not all students need the same amount of practice. Practically speaking, it is much easier to hold students accountable for practicing in smaller groups by orienting them to the task and giving support when things get tough.

Our teaching has the greatest impact when the content and amount of instruction are targeted to each child's needs (Al Otaiba et al., 2011; Connor et al., 2013). We all know some children don't get enough decoding practice. At the same time, though, some children could get too much decoding instruction. In other words, smaller groups allow us to be flexible by providing different amounts of practice. Some children may need more time in smaller groups to get adequate practice; some children will need less time. Some routines, such as Routine 4.5, are quick because practice to improve legibility in letter formation does not take long, while other routines may require more time. Smaller groups allow us to customize the amount of instruction and practice students get to give them what they need.

Smaller groups make it easier to give students immediate, direct feedback.

Immediate, direct feedback is essential when children are acquiring a new skill (Kulik & Kulik, 1988; Wisniewski et al., 2020). We cannot hear and react to all 30 first graders decoding a word written on the board, but we can hear and react to three of them decoding a word while reading in a smaller group.

Without that kind of feedback, children may practice a skill incorrectly and continue making the same errors. Smaller groups allow us to closely monitor each child's performance and offer explicit, timely feedback (Hattie & Timperley, 2007; Oakes et al., 2018; Wisniewski et al., 2020). This not only accelerates learning, but also might boost confidence and motivation (Connor et al., 2014).

Smaller groups bolster the impacts of whole-class instruction.

The most powerful impacts come from combining whole-class and small-group instruction. In two studies, this combined approach was at least two times more effective than whole-class instruction alone (Connor et al., 2014; Reis et al., 2011). In another study, when instructional practices aimed at improving vocabulary and comprehension were aligned in whole-class social studies and small-group reading instruction, struggling readers made greater gains in comprehension (Stevens et al., 2020). Smaller groups that extend whole-class instruction can accelerate the impact of instruction and ensure students have greater access to whole-class content. Here are three ways to connect small-group instruction to whole-class instruction, while still targeting specific needs.

✔ Extend whole-class instruction into more supported practice.

Give students the chance to practice a concept taught in whole-class instruction with more feedback. For example, if first graders are learning about *r*-controlled vowels in whole-class phonics, their learning will be bolstered by more practice reading and spelling words with *r*-controlled vowels in small-group instruction.

✔ Extend whole-class instruction into more independent/partner practice.

To extend this connection even further, consider the time when students are not in a small group: First graders may play a brief game focused on *r*-controlled vowels with a partner. When independent or partner activities are carefully planned to be accessible for learners and connected to their needs, students get even more practice!

✔ Leverage whole-class content-area instruction with topically connected texts.

When students' needs are not aligned with whole-class instruction, particularly in word recognition, instead make a connection to ELA, science, or social studies topics. First graders in the same classroom who are still solidifying a prior phonics skill deserve more supported targeted practice at their point of need, such as reading consonant-vowel-consonant words. But this practice can still connect to whole-class instruction when small-group instruction includes a text. Select a practice text on the same topic as a recent read-aloud, science lesson, or social studies lesson to bolster connections to knowledge-building experiences.

➔ Go here to see Julia explain the purposes of small-group instruction.

ANIMALS ON THE MOVE

Let's see how some animals use their bodies to move from place to place.

Wiggle and Slither

Snakes have no arms, legs, or wings to help them move. They just have their super strong bodies! Snakes are so strong that they are able to pick up their bodies and push or pull forward on their bellies. This wiggling moves them forward and lets them slither across the ground.

Hop, Jump, Dive, and Swim

Frogs are travel masters on land and in water. On land, a frog uses its strong back legs to propel itself forward. It can hop or jump. When a frog is scared or startled, it may quickly dive into a pond, lake, or river. With its webbed feet, a frog can swim well.

Flip and Tumble

The flic-flac spider lives in sandy places, where crawling over dunes can be impossible. But this spider can flip and tumble. It flips its long legs over its body to propel itself up and down the tall sand dunes. Its acrobatic legs help it tumble across the sand, moving twice as fast as most spiders!

SCHOLASTIC

When the content, practice, and teaching moves of small-group instruction are deeply interconnected with the rest of your day, readers have the best chance to grow.

Into the Classroom: Bolstering Whole-Class Instruction With Small Groups

Is it really realistic to connect whole-class instruction to small-group instruction and even independent practice? Teachers near Indianapolis, Indiana, will tell you yes! And, more excitingly, it works! Teachers used an excellent phonics program, but noticed students needed more support. Instead of treating small-group instruction as an island with its own scope and sequence, assessments, and goals, they used small-group instruction to bolster whole-class phonics instruction. They used weekly progress monitoring data in phonics to know who needed more practice in specific skills. Then teachers used routines, particularly those in Chapters 4 and 5, to give targeted, supported practice. Finally, teachers provided yet another chance for students to practice with partner activity and reading focused on the same skills. The results, frankly, speak for themselves. Before targeted small groups, about 40 percent of students were below grade level in phonics. After using targeted small groups, 100 percent of students were at or above grade level.

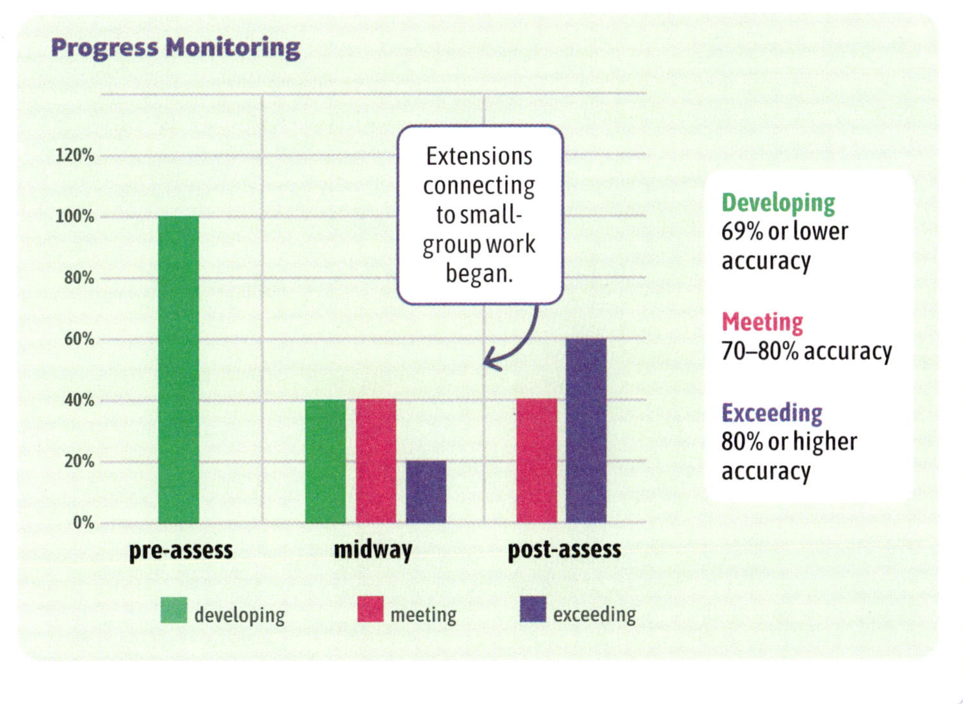

Some Challenges of Small-Group Instruction

It is clear that there are benefits to high-quality small-group instruction. But there are also real challenges that we must keep in mind while weighing costs and benefits.

Small-group instruction is expensive on many levels (Conradi Smith et al., 2022). It is expensive in terms of time: It tends to take more than its fair share of planning time, and can easily take over a literacy block. It is expensive in terms of instruction: Students who are not in a small group may wind up in activities that don't strengthen their literacy skills or, even worse, that may slow their progress. It is expensive in terms of money: Who among us hasn't spent a small fortune on lesson plans, printable books, worksheets, or other activities after scouring the internet for supplemental materials for small groups? Though we can limit those risks, smaller groups are always more expensive than whole-class instruction. But the expense is worth it when small-group instruction is carried out with care.

Furthermore, smaller groups are not inherently better for learning. Evidence-based instruction provided to the whole class can also be incredibly effective (for a phonics example, see Lane et al., 2025). That is particularly true when it comes to developing language comprehension. In fact, one meta-analysis found that vocabulary interventions delivered in whole-class instruction are more effective than those delivered in small groups (Silverman et al., 2020). Research on small-group instruction tends to be stronger for word recognition and fluency (Puzio et al., 2020). That's why I focus most of the routines in this book on developing children's word recognition and fluency. As a rule of thumb, if you can teach something well to the whole class, teach it. Then use small-group time primarily to give children a space to practice what you've taught to the whole class; opportunities for direct, immediate feedback; and/or targeted support based on a specific need.

It is clear that meeting with a smaller group of students gives us the opportunity to support readers in ways that are difficult or impossible within whole-class instruction. It is equally clear that small-group instruction comes with challenges. To maximize the benefits and minimize the challenges, focus on the core purpose of small-group instruction: providing children with targeted, supported practice in exactly what they need to accelerate reading.

In Closing, Remember This Swap...

Less wondering "What should I do with small group?" → More targeted small-group instruction focused on supported practice

We teachers often wonder, "What will I do in small group tomorrow?" Instead, we should wonder, "What do students need to practice with my support?" This mindset swap focuses our thinking on students' needs rather than on filling time in our schedule.

Using small-group instruction with this laser focus on practice means it may look and feel different from how you've taught small groups in the past. Small-group instruction isn't just one thing. A student learning the alphabet does not need to practice reading with expression, and a student strengthening his fluency does not need to practice matching letters to sounds. Small-group instruction changes across reading development to follow the research on the most efficient, effective ways to support different aspects of reading.

To teach targeted small-group instruction, as I've learned from research and from working with educators across the country, we'll begin by exploring reading development and data as ways to identify children's needs. Next, we'll navigate the logistical challenges associated with smaller groups. Then, we'll dive into specific routines that will allow you to provide targeted practice and immediate feedback. Finally, we'll celebrate the incredible growth students can make when they get just what they need to succeed.

CHAPTER 2

Identifying Students' Needs for Small-Group Instruction

In Chapter 1, I discussed how small-group instruction lets us target specific needs by providing more instruction, practice, and support. But, of course, the natural next questions are: How do we know what specific needs children have? And which of those needs should we target with small-group instruction? I aim to answer those questions and others in this chapter.

A Brief Overview of Reading

Let's start with an overview of reading to clarify what I mean by "needs." There are two major components of successful reading: word recognition and language comprehension (Gough & Tunmer, 1986; Scarborough, 2001). When children begin to learn to read, those two components are largely taught and learned separately. As children become fluent readers, they integrate word recognition and language comprehension more. Notice in the graphic on the next page that word recognition moves through four predictable phases but over time becomes more integrated with the ever-growing language comprehension. The result is reading! Let's dive into an overview of the development of word recognition and language comprehension.

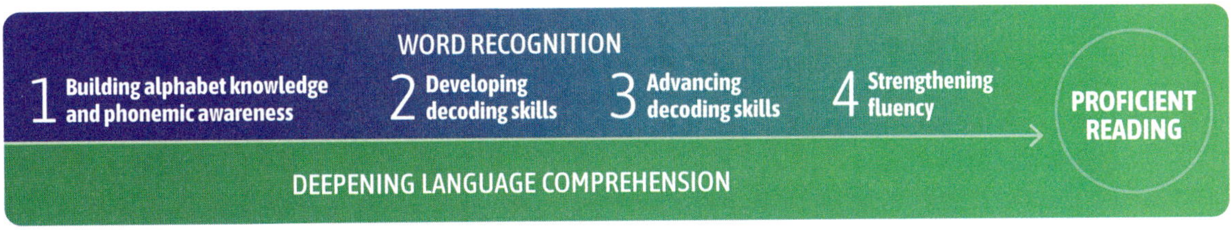

WORD RECOGNITION

1 Building alphabet knowledge and phonemic awareness
2 Developing decoding skills
3 Advancing decoding skills
4 Strengthening fluency

PROFICIENT READING

DEEPENING LANGUAGE COMPREHENSION

Word Recognition

Word recognition develops in predictable, overlapping phases (Ehri, 1995), from recognizing the alphabet and hearing phonemes to strengthening fluency.

Building Alphabet Knowledge and Phonemic Awareness

At the beginning of formal instruction, most children learn the alphabet and gain phonemic awareness. They begin to match letters to sounds to attempt to recognize words. To master that skill, they need a lot of practice with letters and phonemes. It is often best when instruction is direct and straightforward (Roberts & Sadler, 2019).

Into the Classroom: Using Data to Target Phonemic Awareness

Early identification and support make all the difference in children's reading outcomes. For the last two years, one district near Grand Rapids, Michigan, has taken that idea seriously. Led by a tenacious speech-language pathologist, the kindergarten team quickly screens children with a phonemic awareness assessment at the beginning of the year. Children who score in the "at-risk" category receive small-group instruction two times a week for 15 minutes, for a nine-week cycle. Teachers leverage routines that connect phonemes to alphabet learning; focus on identifying, blending, and segmenting sounds; and provide children with tons of practice.

After two nine-week cycles, 59 percent of the kindergartners met grade-level expectations and no longer needed extra support in phonemic awareness. By the end of the year, 98 percent of all kindergartners were on or above grade level! Children measurably improved their phonemic awareness and moved on to other skills. This use of early identification and targeted instruction may seem small, but the impact is big. Many more children are now well on their way to being readers instead of getting stuck at the beginning.

Developing Decoding Skills

As children master the alphabet and gain proficiency in phonemic awareness, they use connections between letters and sounds to fully decode and encode words. Starting from simple CVC words (e.g., *bag*) to words with more sounds/blends (e.g., *brag*) to words with new sounds/digraphs (e.g., *chat*), children read individual sounds across words, and, in the process, expend enormous cognitive effort. But with lots of repetitive practice, the work becomes easier, especially when meaning is attached to the words to ensure students store those words in long-term memory, or "orthographically map" them (Ehri, 1995).

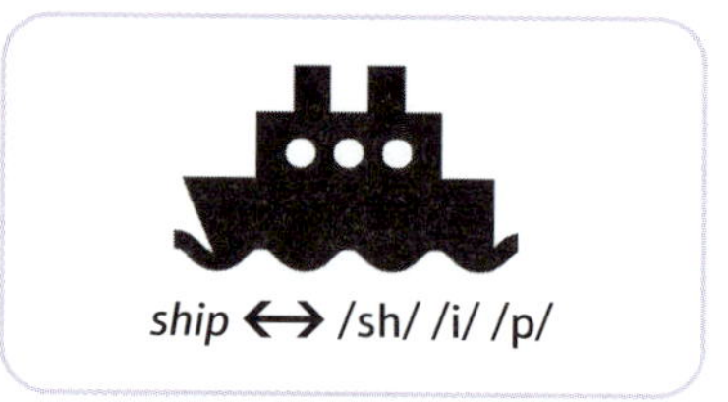

Orthographic map of the word *ship*

Advancing Decoding Skills

With continued explicit instruction, children begin using larger units in words to decode. Instead of reading letter by letter, they process complex vowel patterns, syllables, and even morphemes to decode words. In particular, students learn to notice and use morphemes, which enables them to break large words into decodable parts and understand the words' meanings. Over time, they develop a large vocabulary of "sight words," or words they can recognize immediately, without needing to decode them letter by letter, sound by sound. (According to Brysbaert and colleagues [2016], proficient readers know at least 40,000 words by sight.)

Strengthening Fluency

In time, students should be able to decode well enough to devote more cognitive energy to other aspects of reading. Once they can recognize words automatically and accurately, they should continue to build text-reading fluency, which includes prosody, or reading with expression. Prosody requires proficient word recognition and in-the-moment language comprehension (Wolters et al., 2022). As children continue to engage in supported practice, they become more independent as readers. As fluency grows, they comprehend texts more deeply (Wang et al., 2019).

Into the Classroom: Using Data to Target Fluency

Second-grade teachers near Portland, Oregon, identified student needs in fluency, starting with the one-minute oral reading fluency assessment embedded in their district screener. For children who were accurate, but not necessarily automatic or reading with expression, teachers focused on fluency.

Teachers met with small groups to target fluency with repeated reading and Readers Theater. They carefully crafted fluency lessons to match research and readers' needs.

Teachers also helped readers set clear fluency goals and tracked progress toward goals every other week. Small groups met two to five times a week for about 15 minutes, and, when not in a group, children reread or practiced scripts. "The teaching wasn't perfect, but we were consistent," one teacher said.

After five months (yes, fluency can take time to change), it was time to celebrate. Over 151 students moved from "at risk" into being at grade level or above in fluency, surpassing district goals and everyone's expectations. For these 150 children, the impact can't be understated: They are now readers, ready to take on third grade and beyond.

Language Comprehension

Language comprehension refers to the ability to make sense of spoken or written language, as well as to understandings about vocabulary, syntax, discourse and text structures, inferencing, and background knowledge. It is not as linear, nor as skills-based, as word recognition. We can think of it as a complex braid of knowledge and processes that grows over time, allowing a reader to become increasingly intentional and strategic (Cain et al., 2001; National Reading Panel, 2000; Scarborough, 2001). It is critical for success in reading—improving children's language comprehension is a major goal of education, from preschool through post-graduate experiences.

Early language comprehension development relies primarily on oral experiences. To strengthen and support it, create a language-rich classroom filled with read-alouds, shared readings, and deep conversations that build children's understanding of language and the world through content. In other words, a classroom filled with lots of texts and lots of talk! But much of early language comprehension instruction is outside this book's scope because it's best strengthened and supported by whole-class experiences.

As children's word recognition skills develop, their language comprehension develops, too, from text reading, as well as oral experiences. But learning from texts brings new challenges in language comprehension. Even with adequate word recognition and oral language comprehension, children might need additional support to use their knowledge, skills, and strategies to understand complex texts. That's largely because written language is often quite different from oral language in terms of structure, vocabulary, and syntax (Duke et al., 2021). Some of those needs are discussed in Chapter 8.

What About Children Who Are Learning English?

Children learning English may need different supports, amounts, or intensity of instruction to succeed in reading than their peers (Goldenberg, 2020). It is important to know that English learners are not more likely to have word recognition challenges than their English-first peers (Lesaux et al., 2010). But they are more likely to encounter reading comprehension difficulties (Babayiğit, 2014; Cho et al., 2019). To prevent those difficulties, focus your instruction on oral language, specifically academic language. Oral language interventions can improve the language comprehension of English learners (Roberts et al., 2022).

Though many routines in this book feature elements that are proven to support English learners, I could not provide everything you need to support English learners' oral language development. For more teaching ideas, I recommend the book *Literacy Foundations for English Learners* by Elsa Cárdenas-Hagan, the website ¡Colorín Colorado!, or, for older students, the research-proven CLAVES curriculum by Rebecca Silverman and colleagues.

Targeting Needs With Data

To target needs in small groups, we must have clear data, which allows us to confidently determine what readers know and don't know yet, what they can do and can't do yet. The first step is to identify where children are developmentally when it comes to word recognition. If children are not yet fluent word readers, our first priority must be to ensure they acquire decoding skills (Connor et al., 2009; Harn et al., 2008; Wanzek et al., 2018). That means many children in kindergarten through second grade will be best served by having some small-group instruction dedicated to word recognition and/or fluency support. Beyond second grade, that means we need to quickly identify children who have decoding difficulties. Follow the assessment flowchart on the next page to pinpoint needs across the five skill categories, which appear in the blue boxes.

➔ Go here to see Julia explain how and why data should drive small-group instruction.

Where to start in this chart based on grade level:

- **Kindergarten:** Phonemic awareness and letter-sound knowledge (alphabet)
- **First grade:** Phonemic awareness and letter-sound knowledge (alphabet) or single-syllable decoding
- **Second grade:** Single-syllable decoding
- **Third grade:** Multisyllabic decoding
- **Fourth grade:** Oral reading fluency
- **Fifth grade:** Reading comprehension
- **Above fifth grade:** If you teach older children, I assume you've picked up this book because some of them aren't reading on grade level. Start with an oral reading fluency assessment.

The topic of reading assessment could take up an entire book. In fact, it does! Check out *Reading Assessment Done Right* by Stephanie Stollar and Kate Winn, which contains valuable information on how various types of assessments can help you identify student needs and target your instruction.

Assessment Flowchart to Pinpoint Needs and Target Instruction

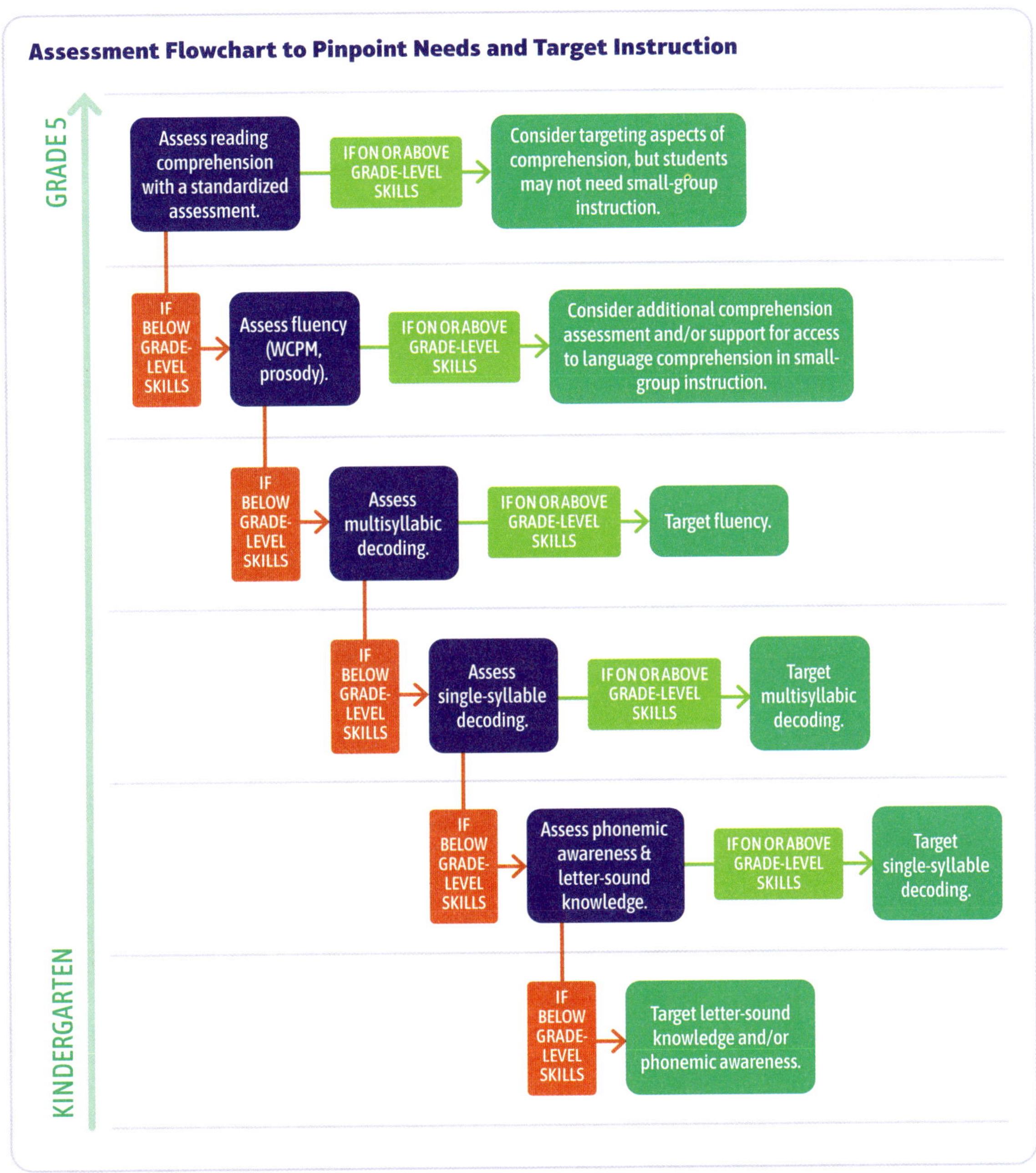

Tips for Alphabet Knowledge and Phonemic Awareness

Assessing alphabet knowledge and phonemic awareness is straightforward. For a basic alphabet assessment, you'll need to show each letter one at a time. You can use letter cards (that do not have images or "hints") or magnetic letters or letter tiles, or just print a piece of paper with all 26 letters in a large, bold font (I like Century Gothic or Poppins).

Basic Alphabet Assessment	Add-On Questions
• Show one lowercase letter at a time and ask, "What sound?" • Score correct or incorrect for each letter.	• Naming: Also ask, "What letter is this?" or "What is the letter's name?" • Uppercase: Show one uppercase letter at a time and ask for the sound and name. • Additional sounds: For *a*, *e*, *i*, *o*, *u*, *c*, *g*: "What's another sound?"

If a student cannot say the sound for a letter within three seconds, consider it wrong. Then record which letters the student identifies incorrectly. Don't record just the total number of letters the student identifies correctly, because then you won't know which letters to target. Plan additional instruction and practice with the missed letters. Repeat this assessment as often as needed.

Don't rely on your screener. Most screening assessments, such as DIBELS/Acadience and NWEA Reading Fluency, do not assess to what extent children know all letters of the alphabet. These assessments are designed to assess children's risk status by comparing their abilities to peers and norms. To do so, they might rely on timed tests (makes it easier to compare across children) or computer-adaptive questioning (to tailor test difficulty). But they generally do not ask children to identify the name and/or sound of all 26 letters. This is a problem for our purposes: Just because a student knows the letter *g*, it does not mean he knows the letter *t*. And we need him to know both! Therefore, I always recommend using a basic paper-and-pencil alphabet test for children learning the alphabet.

To assess phonemic awareness, use 10 three-sound words and ask children to orally blend ("Put these sounds together to make a word") or segment ("Tell me each sound in this word"), starting with words that begin with continuous sounds (*f*, *l*, *m*, *n*, *r*, *s*, *v*, *z*). If children are unable to blend or segment at least seven words, they need practice in phonemic awareness. Note children who struggle to say or hear individual sounds, and plan additional instruction and practice in blending, segmenting, or articulating sounds. Repeat this assessment as often as needed.

Basic Blending Assessment	Basic Segmenting Assessment
I'll say three sounds; you'll put them together, like this: *m e t met.*	I'll say a word; you'll say the sounds, like this: *sat s a t.*
Put these sounds together.	Put these sounds together.
1. m e ss	**1.** zip
2. l a p	**2.** mad
3. s u n	**3.** run
4. t o p	**4.** pot
5. b i d	**5.** ram

Tips for Decoding Single-Syllable and Multisyllabic Words

The first question is, "What kinds of words can this student decode?" To determine children's decoding skills, use a decoding inventory, where children read an increasingly difficult list of words grouped by phonics skills through multisyllabic word features (such as morphemes). For example, children might read 10 CVC words and then 10 words with consonant blends and digraphs. Give the assessment until a student reads words with less than 80 percent accuracy; target decoding practice using words containing phonics patterns she missed.

Decoding Inventories

- Informal Decoding Inventory (IDI)—I recommend this option because it is both free and validated in research; in other words, it accurately identifies what children need to learn (McKenna et al., 2017; Tortorelli et al., 2024). Furthermore, Part II of the IDI is the Multisyllabic Decoding Inventory (MDI). Start here if you are only assessing multisyllabic words.
- CORE Phonics Survey, which includes a Spanish option.
- Your phonics program—check it for a decoding inventory that aligns with instruction. Some programs, such as Really Great Reading, include an inventory.

A second, pressing question in decoding is: "Have students learned what I've taught them—or do they need more practice?" One fast way to assess what children have learned in phonics is through an encoding "check" after teaching a new phonics concept. An encoding check answers the question, "Can children spell words with our new sound-spelling?" If they can spell it, they can decode it! Encoding can also be assessed during whole-class phonics. But this is not a spelling test. Do not send the words home in advance!

Have children spell four words with the target sound-spelling correspondence from your phonics lessons and write one dictated sentence. If 60 percent or more of your students struggle with the task, reteach the target sound-spelling correspondence during whole-class instruction. Otherwise, use small-group instruction to target practice.

Scoring Guidelines for Weekly Encoding Checks

Score words:

- 0–2 correct → more instruction along with more practice in the skill.
- 3 correct → more practice in the skill.
- 4 correct → mastery (continue to review skill to maintain).

Score sentence:

- High-frequency word incorrect (*whut* instead of *what*) → more practice with the word.
- Word with target skill incorrect (*sip* instead of *ship*) → more practice with the skill.
- Word with previous skill incorrect → more review and practice of previous skill.
- Word spelling accurate, but not conventional (*kat* instead of *cat*) → more practice in the skill and direct comparison with spelling options.

You can start with your screener. Start with your school's reliable, valid screening tool for word recognition (for example, DIBELS/Acadience, FastBridge, or Aimsweb; Truckenmiller et al., 2025). Those assessments should give you a good idea about who in your class needs the most support in word recognition, but you will need additional assessment to target specific needs.

Tips for Fluency

To identify students who need support in fluency, use two primary data points: WCPM and scores on a prosody scale.

Words Correct Per Minute (WCPM)

WCPM, or words correct per minute, tells us about accuracy and speed. Ask a student to read aloud a passage from normed assessments. (For informal check-ins, you can use any grade-level passage.) Start timing as soon as the student says the first word. Count or mark the words she does not read accurately within three seconds. Stop the student after one minute and ask her to tell you about what she read. Then count up the number of words the student read correctly in one minute and record the WCPM. If children are reading about 10 WCPM slower than the 50th percentile, they may benefit from additional fluency support or may need additional decoding assessment. Check WCPM progress every other week.

Tips for Getting the Most Accurate WCPM

- Students' background knowledge does impact their fluency (Priebe et al., 2012). Try to pick passages that you are reasonably certain your students can understand.
- In research, oral reading fluency is often measured with the average WCPM of three one-minute readings of three different passages. If you're concerned about the accuracy of one score, just do another quick WCPM assessment with a new passage.

You might not need more than your screener. Oral reading fluency assessments are often embedded in valid screeners (for example, DIBELS/Acadience, FastBridge, or Aimsweb; Truckenmiller et al., 2025). The score is based on the number of words the student reads correctly per minute (WCPM). Follow the steps below to interpret a WCPM score.

Prosody

The second data point relates to children's prosody, or expression while reading aloud. As you measure WCPM, or whenever children are reading, you can also capture prosody information using a scale, such as the Multidimensional Fluency Scale on the next page (Rasinski, 2004; Rasinski & Smith, 2025). This scale asks you to reflect on and score student prosody across dimensions, which research finds is more accurate than scoring prosody as one dimension (Wolters et al., 2022). Students scoring mostly 1s and 2s may benefit from additional fluency support.

Multidimensional Fluency Scale

	4 Excelling	3 Proficient	2 Approaching	1 Developing
E **Expression** ✓ expression matches meaning ✓ varied volume, intonation, and tone ✓ reads with confidence ✓ natural sounding	• consistently uses expression through varied intonation, volume, and tone to match meaning • reads with confidence • is natural-sounding and easy to understand	• mostly uses expression by sometimes varying intonation, volume, and tone to match meaning • shows confidence but inconsistently • is mostly natural-sounding and easy to understand	• attempts expression, but is inconsistent and often does not match the meaning • lacks confidence, reads quietly • primarily focuses on saying the words correctly	• pays minimal or no attention to expression • reads in a quiet and monotone voice • reads words as if simply trying to get them out
A **Automatic Word Recognition** ✓ reads automatically ✓ reads effortlessly ✓ pace matches text (rate)	• reads nearly all words automatically and effortlessly • uses a pace that is consistently conversational and appropriate for the nature of the text • number of words read per minute matches grade-level requirement	• reads most words automatically and effortlessly • uses a mixture of conversational and slow reading • number of words read per minute meets grade-level requirement	• does not read most words automatically and has to stop to recognize words • reads at a moderately slow pace • number of words read per minute is below grade-level requirement	• does not read words automatically and has to stop frequently to recognize words • reads at an excessively slow and laborious pace • number of words read is well below grade-level requirement
R **Rhythm and Phrasing** ✓ reads phrase-by-phrase chunks ✓ attention to punctuation with intonation and pauses ✓ easy to listen to	• reads primarily in phrases, chunks, and sentence units • pays attention to intonation and pauses at punctuation consistently and accurately	• reads with some choppiness, but is generally able to go phrase by phrase • pays attention to intonation and usually pauses at punctuation consistently and accurately	• reads in two- and three-word phrases frequently • reads with choppiness • often exhibits improper intonation and pauses at punctuation	• reads word by word frequently • reads in a monotone manner • shows little sense of phrase boundaries • exhibits improper intonation and pauses at punctuation
S **Smoothness** ✓ smooth-sounding with flow ✓ accurate word recognition ✓ minimal hesitations ✓ self-corrects	• reads nearly all words accurately • reads smoothly, with minimal hesitations • has few word and structure difficulties and corrects quickly	• reads most words accurately • breaks occasionally from smoothness and hesitates • has a few difficulties with specific words and/or structures, but they do not impede overall flow	• struggles to read words accurately • pauses and hesitates frequently at "rough spots" in text, which disrupts the overall flow	• requires frequent assistance for inaccuracies: long pauses, insertions, mispronunciations, omissions, false starts, sound-outs, and repetitions • is unaware of mistakes

(Rasinski & Smith, 2025)

Tips for Language Comprehension

To understand more about children's language comprehension, I'll focus on three areas that you can easily assess as you're teaching: vocabulary, syntax, and text structure. All of these assessments can be for language comprehension (with a sentence or text read aloud) or reading comprehension (with the student reading a sentence or text). These are not the only areas of comprehension you can assess, but they'll give you a good starting point to determine which routines may be helpful.

Knowledge of Text Content

You can assess children's retelling of a narrative text using a rubric (Petersen et al., 2017), such as Language Dynamics Group's Narrative Language Measure, which you can download for free on its website. You read a story to the student, ask her to retell it, and then score her performance based on story grammar, language complexity, and retell. You can also use this structure to create your own retell assessments with texts that are familiar to students. If children's retells are out of order, not detailed, or missing key information, they may benefit from more support in understanding how to retell complex texts.

Knowledge of Vocabulary

We can also assess children's language comprehension through vocabulary acquisition. In addition to standardized testing of vocabulary (using, for example, a screener) and testing children on words you've taught, you can assess children's ability to infer meanings of new words (Wise & Duke, 2025). If children cannot tell the meanings of new words, they may benefit from additional support and strategies to do so.

How to Know If a Student Has Difficulty Recognizing Word Meanings

Follow this sequence:

- **Read a sentence:** The garage was dingy. It was full of trash. "What does *dingy* mean?"
- **Ask a follow-up question with options:** "Does *dingy* mean bright or dirty?"

Knowledge of Sentence-Level Content

Finally, you can assess how children understand sentences. Children's ability to understand complex sentences accounts for differences in their ability to understand texts (Poulsen & Gravgaard, 2016; Zipoli, 2017). With young children, use games such as Simon Says to informally assess sentence comprehension:

"Simon says... touch your head after you clap your hands." With older children, check on sentence comprehension during reading. For example, they may come upon a sentence in passive voice ("The criminal was captured by the sheriff"). Pause and ask children to retell the sentence or say who was captured. Children who have a hard time following complex syntax may need more support navigating sentences.

Consider a valid, reliable screener. Language comprehension is notoriously challenging to assess accurately. It is highly reliant on background knowledge, which varies from person to person and from assessment to assessment. Though they have many flaws, screeners that assess elements of language comprehension can identify children who are at risk (for example, DIBELS/Acadience, easyCBM, and i-Ready; Truckenmiller et al., 2025). Beyond those screeners, focus on assessing children's comprehension within topic areas you have taught. If you have significant concerns about a child's language development, connect with your school's speech and language professionals.

What This Book Will Help You Target

This kind of assessment data helps you answer key questions: How do I know what specific needs children have? And which of those needs should I target with small-group instruction? Beyond that, however, you often need to get even more specific. It's one thing to say, "Research says you can effectively target decoding skills in small-group instruction," but that's not helpful if you're wondering, "What do I do with this student who keeps mixing up short *i* and *e*?"

As children learn to read, they encounter predictable challenges. Some of them are big: A student might have difficulty decoding words, over and over again, even with lots of instruction and support. Some of them are small, but still can prevent progress: A student might be making great progress learning the alphabet, but get stuck trying to blend three sounds into a CVC word. Often, great resources for meeting those smaller needs are hard to find. Standard advice is too often "They need more," but it isn't always clear what "more" is.

Small Groups, Big Results focuses on some of the small but common needs in reading that can be efficiently and effectively taught using research-based practices. Those challenges come from questions I hear from teachers, research, and my personal experiences with students.

Target Element	Specific Challenge	Routine
Alphabet Knowledge	Automaticity in letter sounds	4.1
Phonemic Awareness	Discriminating and articulating phonemes	4.2
	Blending three sounds	4.3
	Segmenting three sounds	4.4
Handwriting (Bonus! See box below.)	Forming letters legibly	4.5
Decoding Skills	Basic decoding in context	5.1
	Decoding in knowledge-building contexts	5.2
	Typically confusing vowel sounds and spellings	5.3
	Decoding and encoding words with more than three sounds	5.4
	Accuracy and automaticity of irregular high-frequency words	5.5
Advanced Decoding Skills and Morphology	Reading two-syllable words using syllables	6.1
	Chunking multisyllabic words in texts	6.2
	Chunking multisyllabic words with affixes	6.3
	Recognizing vowels and pronouncing them	6.4
Fluency	Reading at an appropriate pace	7.1
	Phrasing when reading text aloud	7.2
	Expression when reading text aloud	7.3
Language Comprehension	Understanding unknown words	8.1
	Navigating complex syntax	8.2
	Understanding text structure	8.3
	Generating inferences	8.4

What Is Handwriting Doing Here?

For two good reasons:

It is a common area of need. With up to 30 percent of children struggling to write legibly, handwriting experts have increasingly called for devoting more instructional time to handwriting (Bonneton-Botté et al., 2023). Research finds that about 10 hours of instruction leads to considerable improvements in legibility (Graham & Harris, 2018). That's only about three minutes a day.

It is necessary for literacy development. Even in our digital age, children need legible handwriting because it contributes to literacy development. First, while children learn the alphabet, forming letters can strengthen letter name and sound knowledge (Ray et al., 2022). Handwriting also predicts children's growth in spelling (Pritchard et al., 2021). Second, handwriting is critical for succeeding in writing. When children are able to write legibly and efficiently, their writing improves (based on writing quality, writing fluency, and length of writing; Santangelo & Graham, 2016).

In Closing, Remember This Swap...

Less "catch all" small-group instruction → More targeted small-group instruction based on research and data

I wrote this chapter to clarify what small-group instruction should target. By focusing on understanding how reading develops, through the phases of word recognition and the strengthening of language comprehension, I aimed to give you the information you need to pinpoint skills children need to become proficient readers. Use data to target the specific needs of readers. Whether a student is stuck blending CVC words, reading too slowly, or confused by complex syntax, the goal is the same: Use clear, targeted data to guide your teaching. When you do, small-group instruction is more purposeful and powerful.

CHAPTER 3

The "Big 10" Questions About Small-Group Instruction

Planning is key to the success of your small-group instruction, and part of that means taking into consideration all the realities of your school and classroom. If you have a strict MTSS system, you need to plan differently than if you are pretty much working on your own. If you teach in a multigrade classroom, you likely have a larger range of needs to plan for than if you teach just one grade level. To help you with the logistics of small-group instruction, this chapter focuses on answering the 10 biggest questions educators ask me.

The "Big 10" Questions About Small-Group Instruction

- How can data help me plan instruction?
- How much time should I dedicate to small-group instruction?
- What about typical teaching constraints? How can I structure small-group instruction within them?
- How do I group students?
- What does a small-group lesson look like?
- How do I plan for small-group lessons?
- What materials am I going to need?
- How do I know if my instruction is working?
- What in the world are the other kids doing?
- How can an administrator support small-group instruction?

QUESTION 1: **How can data help me plan instruction?**

You can use data to get clear, specific answers to questions such as:

- What phase of word reading is the student in? ("Charlie is developing decoding skills.")
- What does he need to practice to get to the next phase of word reading or to improve comprehension? ("He needs to practice decoding words in texts and tends to be ready to practice with the skills along our first-grade phonics scope and sequence.")
- Which, if any, skills is he getting stuck on? ("Specifically, he also needs some extra practice on a prior skill: not skipping sounds in words with consonant blends.")

Once you've asked these questions of all your students, you can make a clear plan for practice in small groups, such as: "Charlie will be in a group reading a decodable text matched to our scope and sequence one to two times a week (Routines 5.1 and 5.2). He'll also be in a group focused on not skipping sounds (Routine 5.4) one to two times a week until he is encoding words with consonant blends correctly 90 percent of the time." In that way, small-group instruction is based on the categories children are in and the practices they need to grow as readers. For more on determining students' needs, see Chapter 2.

Category	What Students Need to Practice	Grades
Building Alphabet Knowledge and Phonemic Awareness	• Hearing, saying, blending, and segmenting phonemes. • Matching letter forms to sounds and names.	PK, K, 1
Developing Decoding Skills	• Decoding and encoding words with increasingly complex sound-spelling correspondences, including irregular high-frequency words. • Connecting decoded words to their meanings by reading them in context.	K, 1, 2
Advancing Decoding Skills	• Chunking words into parts via syllables, morphemes, or patterns to decode. • Connecting morphemes to meanings of words. • Connecting decoded words to their meanings by reading them in context.	1, 2, 3
Strengthening Fluency	• Reading with sufficient speed. • Reading with attention toward prosody (phrasing, expression, and smoothness).	2+
Deepening Language Comprehension With Complex Texts*	• Using text structure in retellings and to understand texts more deeply. • Determining the meanings of unknown words in texts using morphology and context. • Navigating complex syntax and generating inferences.	2+

*Remember, language comprehension does not follow word recognition. It must be supported throughout school. The final category in this book does not focus on all aspects of language comprehension, but rather focuses on routines to improve readers' language comprehension in order to access complex texts. These routines will be most impactful after decoding skills are solidified.

QUESTION 2: **How much time should I dedicate to small-group instruction?**

There is one rather unsettling fact that must be considered when deciding how much time to dedicate to small-group instruction: Children who need the most amount of time with teacher-led instruction are the same children who cannot productively spend much time in student-managed activities. That is another reason to maximize your whole-class instructional time! To attempt to split the difference, I suggest the basic schedule below.

Most children in the class fall into the ___ category	Total time in small-group instruction / with some children in student-managed activities	Number of small groups with direct, teacher-led instruction
Alphabet Knowledge and Phonemic Awareness	20 minutes/day	Example: two 10-minute groups/day
Developing Decoding Skills	30 minutes/day	Example: three 10-minute groups/day
Advancing Decoding Skills	20–30 minutes/day	Example: two 15-minute groups/day
Strengthening Fluency	10–30 minutes/day	Example: two 15-minute groups/day
Deepening Language Comprehension With Complex Texts	Highly dependent on needs. You may need to meet with only one group per day as most instruction should occur with the whole class.	

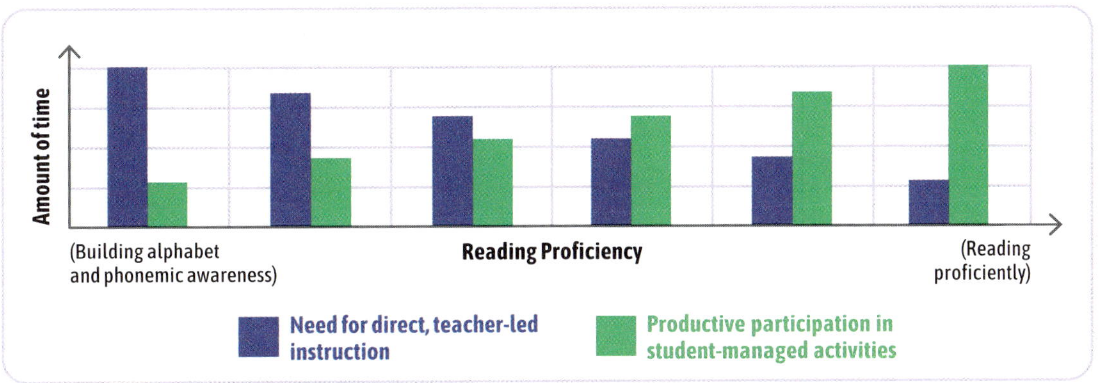

QUESTION 3: **What about typical teaching constraints? How can I structure small-group instruction within them?**

Below are some constraints that you likely encounter in your school, and how to work within them. It is important to know that, as of this writing, research does not clearly indicate the best way to structure small groups. If you aren't sure how to structure your groups, try one or two of these ideas and adjust it to fit the reality of your students, class, and school.

If You Have This Constraint...	Try This...
You teach young children and need to limit the amount of time they are doing independent activities.	Instead of one longer block of time to meet with two small groups, have two shorter blocks, 7–10 minutes each. During each block, meet with one group while other students engage in a short activity.
You have some children with needs that are two grade levels below your grade level, but many students who are on track.	Instead of meeting with all students the same number of times per week, plan to meet with the group(s) with the highest needs more frequently, even if the students are receiving additional intervention outside your classroom. Plan to meet with groups that are "on track" with whole-class instruction perhaps one to two times a week, and students who aren't three to five times a week.
You are expected to meet with every group every day, but some children need way less support than others.	Instead of meeting with all children for the same amount of time each day, vary the amount of time. For example, engage some groups in an entire decoding routine (10–15 minutes), and have other groups join you to read just one page of a decodable and continue reading in pairs.
You are expected to carry out small-group instruction during one 30-minute block (part of a whole-school schedule) and need help using it flexibly.	Instead of having children rotate, give them tasks to complete and then call children to your table. In other words, use this time flexibly! If one group only lasts 7 minutes (such as Routine 4.1), it will not "mess up" other children's rotations.
You want the other students to read independently, but they are not actually reading.	Instead of choice reading, have children engage in SPORT reading to improve their fluency even without small-group instruction (see Chapter 7).

QUESTION 4: **How do I group students?**

Put children into groups of no more than five, based on the category of their needs (word reading phases or comprehension) (Lou et al., 1996). To create groups, consider your data. For example, for the alphabet knowledge and phonemic awareness category, don't group children based on the number of letters they don't know. Instead, group them based on the specific letters they don't know. That way, you'll be able to target instruction much more easily.

One of the biggest critiques of small-group instruction is that it can essentially "track" children into low-, middle-, and high-performing groups, which can reduce children's motivation to read and prevent them from learning from their peers (as described by Siegal et al., 2024). So, be flexible in two ways:

- First, assign children to more than one group. One group does not need to meet every need a student has, nor should it. Consider this scenario: Carlos, Sophia, Aiden, and Liam are in a group targeting alphabet knowledge. You meet with this group two times a week using Routine 4.1. But Carlos also needs support saying certain English phonemes. He also joins a group focused on articulating phonemes (Routine 4.2) that meets once a week.
- Second, rotate children to new groups regularly. Researchers recommend updating groups when children's needs change (Castle et al., 2005). Some children in a group might respond faster than others to instruction. Some children may have a new and different need from their groupmates. While there isn't a precise answer from research, I recommend adjusting groups at least once every six weeks.

For details about grouping for each skill category, check out the introductions to Chapters 4–8.

QUESTION 5: **What does a small-group lesson look like?**

Select the best routines to meet your students' needs from Chapters 4 to 8. It may seem like a lot of options at first! But you'll quickly see that the routines share a lot in common in terms of structure. They are all between 5 minutes and 15 minutes long, and each one follows the same steps:

- **Review:** Time to review gives children practice with prior skills or the chance to activate background knowledge.
- **Teach:** Explicit instruction ensures children get more of what they need: clear information and modeling. It is especially important if children are struggling to learn a particular skill.

- **Practice and Application:** The "secret sauce" of small-group instruction is tons of opportunities to practice the skill in either (1) constrained tasks or (2) within texts. In both cases, children need lots of supportive, immediate feedback.
    - I use the term "Practice" for constrained tasks or activities. In Practice activities, children do *only* the target skill; for example, pointing at a letter tile and saying the sound.
    - I use the term "Application" for tasks within texts (reading or writing). In Application activities, children need to use the target skill within context; for example, decoding words within a decodable text.
    - You'll notice that the routines focus more heavily on practice when children are at the early phases of word recognition and more heavily on application when children have more skills.
- **Prompt:** Each routine also comes with its own guide to supercharge feedback, a crucial component.

Each routine is filled with research-based suggestions for language to use, practice opportunities to provide, and application activities to do with children. It even offers ways to increase or decrease the rigor, depending on how your students are responding to the instruction. I recommend starting with one or two routines that feel familiar and meet the needs of your students. Once you feel good with those, branch out.

→ Go here to see Julia explain what a small-group lesson should look like.

I Want Print-and-Go Resources!

That's reasonable. Here are some free or low-cost resources that support the ideas in this book, all created by researchers.

- **All categories:** Differentiated Instruction in Bookworms (K–5) by Walpole and McKenna
- **Word recognition only:** UFLI Foundations Toolbox and Project Read AI by Lane and Contesse
- **Multisyllabic word recognition:** *Word Connections* by Toste
- **Fluency:** *The Megabook of Fluency, Second Edition*, by Rasinski and Smith
- **Oral language/English learners:** CLAVES curriculum by Silverman and colleagues

QUESTION 6: **How do I plan for small-group lessons?**

To plan for small-group lessons, you'll need two pieces of information.

First, you need to know exactly what children need to learn and/or practice. This informs the routine you pick from Chapters 4 to 8, the explicit instruction you need to give, and the practice activities to choose.

Second, if the routine includes text reading, you need to know what children are learning in ELA, science, or social studies. That way, you can select a topically related text to ensure that your small-group instruction connects to your content-area instruction and is helping to build your students' knowledge.

So grab your student data, open up to the routine that matches the needs it reveals, and make a content connection! At right is an example of a plan for increasing second graders' reading speed to improve fluency. Check out Routine 7.1 for more on this.

Group	Camila, Brian, Divya
Routine	**7.1** How to improve reading at an appropriate pace
Skill Need	This group is focused on improving their pace while reading. **Fall 2nd grade goal: 50 WCPM** Camila: 37 WCPM Brian: 30 WCPM Divya: 40 WCPM
Content Connection	We're studying fossils in our ELA module, so we'll read a passage from ____.
Review	Chorally read the passage from last session, ____.
Explicit Instruction	Remind students of goal right now of increasing speed (by 10 percent). Camila: 41 WCPM Brian: 33 WCPM Divya: 44 WCPM Model reading.
Practice	Chorally read two times. Text-dependent question: "____?"
Application	Release to keep reading the rest of the book in partnerships.

Moving From a Routine to a Lesson Plan

This book provides routines, but not lesson plans in the traditional sense. To go from routine to plan, you'll need to determine your teaching point and customize the content. For example, you'll need a lot of word lists for children to practice decoding. To create the best word list, include words with the target phonics skill (for example, words with *-ck*) and some words with previously learned phonics skills (for example, CVC words). This helps children get more distributed practice, meaning practice in a skill over time, not just at one time (Seabrook et al., 2005). Aim for about 50 percent of words to have the target skill and 50 percent to include previously learned content (Burns et al., 2004).

QUESTION 7: **What materials am I going to need?**

Here is a list of materials for all routines in the book. Don't let the length of the list scare you! Look at each item—I bet you already have most of them.

Category	Student Materials
Building Alphabet Knowledge and Phonemic Awareness	• Alphabet cards • Magnetic letters or letter tiles • Alphabet books • Sound/word boxes • Articulation cards • Pictures of key words • Handheld mirrors • Whiteboards • Paper with handwriting lines • Letter stroke cards
Developing Decoding Skills	• Decodable texts • Word lists printed on a single sheet or cut out, depending on activity • Sound/word boxes • Writing paper or whiteboards • Vowel cards or chart • Dice • Magnetic letters • Pictures of key vocabulary words
Advancing Decoding Skills	• Grade-level passages or texts • Word lists • Morpheme cards • Maze sentences • Vowel cards or chart
Strengthening Fluency	• Grade-level passages or texts • Goal-setting chart • Phrase list • An audience! (for Readers Theater)
Deepening Language Comprehension With Complex Texts	• Grade-level passages or texts • Highlighters • Writing paper • Morpheme cards • Maze sentences • Sentence list • Graphic organizers What the Text Says / What I Know / What I Can Infer

QUESTION 8: **How do I know if my instruction is working?**

To monitor children's progress, use the progress monitoring assessments listed in Chapter 2 for each category. Those assessments will give you a broad understanding of how children's skills are changing over time.

I also recommend informally monitoring children's progress during your lessons. Aim to record children's performance every three to five lessons. For example, you might jot down how many words each student in a group decoded correctly during practice. You don't need formal assessments; just keep track of how children do during instruction.

Here's an example: You have a group of four kindergartners who are struggling to blend three-sound words. On an initial assessment of 10 words, they all score zero. After three blending-focused lessons (Routine 4.3), give an informal assessment during the Practice step of your lesson by asking children to blend words one at a time instead of all together. Write down how many words each student could blend. If it's more than zero, then, yes, your instruction is working! If it is five to seven words in a row, the student is ready to move on to a more rigorous skill.

QUESTION 9: **What in the world are the other kids doing?**

Every time I speak with teachers about small-group instruction, this is the number-one question. It is a critical question, and the answer has as much to do with managing behavior as it does about learning.

Children need explicit instruction and teacher-supported practice to master word recognition skills. So our focus should be on making the most of the moments we are in front of children. Even when children are engaged in learning-focused activities, it is highly unlikely that student-managed time is more productive than teacher-led time. To make the most of student-managed time, consider what children are able to practice on their own or with a partner. In Chapters 4–8, I offer some ideas for children in each category, including:

- Structured games, such as those available for free from the Florida Center for Reading Research, to target specific skills.
- Research-supported tech products.
- Decodable text reading.
- For children gaining fluency: Topically connected text reading.
- Writing about reading.

Beyond those activities, I invite you to think creatively. There is no rule that says children can't work on a math activity, engage in a productive discussion with a peer, or spend a few minutes looking at a book they can't read yet. Indeed, some children may benefit from having a couple of minutes to relax before moving on to another activity. I know that may sound sacrilegious, but it's exhausting to engage in intense cognitive learning every second of the day. In other words, it is okay if a tiny part of small-group time is not the productive moment of the day, as long as the amount of time is brief and students are also receiving targeted, high-quality instruction.

To Rotate or Not to Rotate?

A lot of teachers organize small-group instruction by having children stay in groups and rotate between centers and the teacher table. Instead, try keeping the teacher table out of the rotations. When you are ready for a group, call over the students in it to start your lesson. This will allow you to:

- Group children for independent work in ways that help keep the classroom calm, rather than trying to match specific needs—which can sometimes stir things up more than help.
- Teach lessons for varying amounts of time. You can pull a group to practice handwriting for four minutes and another group to read a decodable text for 10 minutes without disrupting other activities.
- Occasionally skip a group and circulate around the classroom to give children feedback and support during independent work.

QUESTION 10: **How can an administrator support small-group instruction?**

If you are an administrator, the best way you can support small-group instruction is to ensure teachers have what they need to actually meet students' needs. To do this, I recommend reflecting on the following critical questions.

1. Broadly, how is our school doing? Ways to answer this question:

- List all the literacy assessments your school administers and what each assessment tells you. Across assessments and grade levels, how many students are deemed at risk? Does this number increase or decrease over grade levels?

If more than 50 percent of your school is scoring in the at-risk category on valid, reliable assessments of reading, I strongly encourage you to focus on improving whole-class instruction and/or choose a whole-school structure for small-group instruction, such as Success for All and high-quality versions of MTSS.

2. How are teachers currently carrying out small-group instruction? Ways to answer these questions:

- Ask teachers in a nonjudgmental, nonevaluative way to describe if, when, and how they use small-group instruction.
- Observe small-group instruction, outside of evaluations, to better understand.

Use reality as your starting point. If teachers are not using small-group instruction at all, consider starting with conversations or a book study. (You're holding a book that might be a good choice!)

3. What resources do teachers have to implement small-group instruction? What do teachers say they need? Ways to answer these questions:
    - Ask teachers! If they say, "We don't have enough decodable texts," buy more decodable texts!
    - Look through your curricular resources and consider how they support small-group instruction—and how they don't.

See Question 7 for resources teachers may need.

In Closing, Remember This Swap

Less fidelity to one program → More fidelity to children and data

I hear all the time from teachers and administrators that they want to use their Tier-1 program "with fidelity," meaning they want to use the program exactly as written to ensure children learn. There are several challenges with that idea.

- First, many programs have never been studied in research, so there is no guarantee that using a program with fidelity will lead to particular outcomes.
- Second, the program adopted does not matter as much as the instructional practices that teachers use when implementing the program (Slavin et al., 2011).
- Third, most programs include virtually no built-in opportunities to differentiate instruction based on specific skills. For example, one widely used core literacy program includes three small-group reading lesson plans per week for "low, on grade level, and high" readers—designations that are likely too vague to precisely support needs.

To meet readers' needs, it is essential to focus on research-based practices and respond to children's data. This often means that we need to strengthen Tier-1 programs with targeted, differentiated support. When indicated by data, adding additional targeted small-group instruction means students will have more opportunities to learn than if we are overly concerned with using one program precisely as written.

CHAPTER 4

Building Alphabet Knowledge and Phonemic Awareness

Children who are developing alphabet knowledge and phonemic awareness are in the earliest moments of word recognition. When we're working with children at this phase, we're helping them understand how letters can represent sounds. Though those skills do not develop in a lockstep fashion, they are linked. Both are key predictors of long-term literacy outcomes (Caravolas et al., 2019).

The goal of instruction is to move students toward decoding and encoding (spelling). For that to happen, children need to know:

- Letters represent sounds.
- Specific letters, such as *d*, represent specific sounds, such as /d/.
- We can blend sounds together to say words.
- We can say individual sounds to segment words.

Though children do not need to master any of those skills to begin developing decoding and encoding skills, they do need sufficient knowledge of the alphabet and phonemes to read and spell words (Ehri, 2014; Hulme & Snowling, 2013). The routines explained later in this chapter will help you do that.

What Do Children Need to Practice?

To solidify alphabet knowledge and phonemic awareness, children need practice in:

- **Saying individual phonemes.** Children can get stuck on certain phonemes, particularly if they are new to English. More explicit instruction in articulation may help (Routine 4.2).
- **Recognizing the names, sounds, and formations of letters.** Children can get stuck on certain alphabet letter names and sounds. Lots of additional, supported practice can help (Routine 4.1).
- **Blending sounds together to say words.** Many children have a hard time blending three sounds, an essential skill to move into decoding consonant-vowel-consonant (CVC) words. A more scaffolded blending strategy may help move them toward decoding (Routine 4.3).
- **Segmenting sounds from words.** Children can also get stuck trying to segment three sounds, an essential skill to move into encoding CVC words. Supported practice using manipulatives can help progress (Routine 4.4).

All of those skills have oral components, and, like all skills with oral components, it can be challenging to hold all children accountable for practice and give adequate feedback to the whole class. When one student out of a class of 26 decides to just mouth the answer, it is often difficult to distinguish that child's response and provide support. Every student learning the alphabet and developing phonemic awareness benefits from practice and feedback in a smaller group.

Don't Overlook Handwriting!

To encode words and become a writer, children need legible handwriting—and that starts with clear, efficient letter formation (Santangelo & Graham, 2016). All children need practice forming letters, with direct feedback and, as necessary, correction to solidify their skills (Routine 4.5).

Logistics of Small-Group Instruction to Build Alphabet Knowledge and Phonemic Awareness

Let me be frank: It's the logistics that really matter! These are the most common questions I get about building alphabet knowledge and phonemic awareness in small groups:

- When should I start small groups?
- How do I group children and plan a week?
- How much time do I need?
- What should children do when they aren't in small groups?

When should I start small groups?

The short answer: as soon as you can, especially if you've identified children who need more support than you can provide in whole-class instruction. If your school provides support systems only through time-consuming formal assessment processes, timely small-group instruction is particularly important.

How do I group children and plan a week?

Research-tested small-group instruction for alphabet knowledge and phonemic awareness tends to include about three to five students (Roberts, 2021).

- For alphabet skills, group children based on letter sounds they don't know, not on the number of letter-sounds they are missing. Create flexible groups to accommodate children who are missing different letters from peers.
- For phonemic awareness skills, group children based on their area of need: identification, blending, or segmenting.

If children are struggling with both alphabet knowledge and phonemic awareness, consider placing them in multiple targeted groups.

How much time do I need?

The routines to support alphabet knowledge and phonemic awareness are quick, just 5–10 minutes each. Though there is not a clear answer to the question, "How many sessions per week?" researchers reiterate that groups should be changing based on skill acquisition. Most children in this phase need an opportunity to practice, with your direct support in a small group. On the next page is a sample week of small-group instruction for children with a variety of needs.

A Sample Week of Small-Group Instruction

Caleb is struggling with letter sounds and formations. Nicola is also struggling with letter sounds and is bilingual, sometimes confusing similar sounds. Sebastian has solid letter knowledge but is working on phonemic awareness skills. Notice how sometimes they are in the same small group but not always, because the groups are flexible, based on their individual needs.

	Monday	Tuesday	Wednesday	Thursday	Friday
Caleb	Letter group (Routine 4.1, page 55)	No small group	Letter group (Routine 4.1, page 55)	Handwriting group (Routine 4.5, page 69)	Letter group (Routine 4.1, page 55)
Nicola	No small group	Articulation group (Routine 4.2, page 58)	Letter group (Routine 4.1, page 55)	Articulation group (Routine 4.2, page 58)	Letter group (Routine 4.1, page 55)
Sebastian	Blending group (Routine 4.3, page 62)	Articulation group (Routine 4.2, page 58)	Blending group (Routine 4.3, page 62)	No small group	Segmenting group (Routine 4.4, page 65)

What should children do when they aren't in small groups?

When students aren't working with you directly, they should practice skills that they can successfully accomplish on their own by engaging in the activities described below. Be attentive to time; we shouldn't expect young children to engage in these independent tasks for more than about 10 minutes at a time.

Games. After playing a game during small-group instruction, students can continue playing it in pairs. Match the Sound is a good choice! Here is an example with first sound identification. This game can also be played with middle and ending sounds and to spell or read whole words as students' skills increase.

Materials needed

- Pictures of items that start with target sounds; for example, *cat*, *hen*, *mop*, *pig*, *rug*, and *van*.
- Magnet letters for each target sound: *c*, *h*, *m*, *p*, and *v*.

Partner A: Selects a picture and says the word.
Partner B: Says the first sound and picks the letter.
Partner A: Agrees or disagrees.
Then switch roles.

For more game ideas, I recommend the Florida Center for Reading Research Student Center Activities.

Tech Tools. In a meta-analysis, Rice and her colleagues (2022) found that tech-supported phonemic awareness practice can be effective. They reviewed research on three tools: GraphoGame, Lexia, and Waterford. Students can use those tools for short periods of time to continue practicing phonemic awareness. For alphabet knowledge, look for tools that enable students to practice hearing and using letter sounds, not just names.

Books. Students can look at alphabet books or familiar picture books. Encourage them to "read" known letters when they see them by pointing at the letter and saying its sound. Looking at books before being able to read does not negatively impact students' literacy development.

Ebooks With Audio. Though most ebooks don't directly support alphabet knowledge or phonemic awareness, students will likely enjoy hearing narrative and informational text read fluently, on their own. Choose ebooks that connect to your ELA, science, and/or social studies lessons to bolster oral language development and background knowledge.

Step-by-Step Routines for Building Alphabet Knowledge and Phonemic Awareness

Children need a lot of practice to solidify their alphabet knowledge and phonemic awareness. These five routines will help you target areas where students need more support and practice. Each one follows research-based principles, with clear, explicit directions, specific practice and application opportunities, and examples of direct feedback you might give to students. The routines are not meant to be taught in order; use them as students need them.

➔ Go here to see a video demonstration of a Chapter 4 routine in action.

➔ Go here for downloadable resources for these Chapter 4 routines.

4.1 How to Support Automaticity in Letter Sounds

Purpose: To support children in automatically recalling letter sounds by giving them targeted, repetitive practice.

Problem This Routine Solves

To use alphabet knowledge to decode, children must accurately match letters to sounds and automatically match letters to sounds. Children may know that *f* spells /f/—but if they have to stop and think about it, decoding is slow and frustrating. Some children struggle to gain this level of automaticity with letter sounds. Though research indicates children should learn letter names and sounds simultaneously (Roberts, 2021), it is far more important for them to gain automaticity with letter sounds in order to decode and encode.

Does this sound familiar?

Children who aren't automatic with letter sounds may:

- Be unable to articulate the sound for a letter.
- Need more than three seconds to articulate the sound for a letter.
- Articulate letter sounds when looking at letters in isolation, but not within a word.
- Still be learning the alphabet! Even children keeping up with whole-class instruction need brief check-ins so that you can give them precise feedback.

What the Research Says

To gain automaticity, children need a few basic things: explicit instruction, an enormous amount of practice, and direct feedback from you. One of the most effective aspects of alphabet learning is paired associate learning (PAL): having students repeatedly match a letter with its sound or name. Even without letter formation, letter articulation, or other common aspects of alphabet instruction, PAL protocols lead to the optimum learning outcomes (Roberts, 2021)—most importantly, helping children identify letters more quickly. I know it doesn't sound fancy, but it works!

Children need an enormous amount of practice pairing letters to sounds to gain alphabet knowledge. While crafting lessons to teach the alphabet for studies, Fitzgerald and her colleagues (2020) gave children over 60 chances to pair a letter with its sound to ensure learning. That shows just how much practice children likely need to learn the alphabet.

Materials

- Alphabet cards connected to your phonics lessons
- Magnetic letters or letter tiles (select 4–8 letters you have taught, along with a new target letter)
- Alphabet book or large-print passage containing the new target letter

Routine (7–10 minutes)

Review. Review letter-sound correspondences you've taught by showing a letter card and having children name the letter and say its sound.

Teach. To teach a new letter or remind children of a letter you've taught, use clear, explicit language: "This is the letter *b*. *B* spells the sound /b/. We can hear the sound /b/ at the beginning of *ball*. Say *b*. Say /b/."

Practice and Apply. All activities should focus on children either seeing a letter and saying its sound or hearing a sound and selecting its corresponding letter. Don't be afraid of repetition! By repeatedly practicing target letter sounds, children will develop automaticity. Aim for at least 15 practice or application opportunities with the target letter sound per lesson, but keep the lesson short, under 10 minutes, particularly for children who are also struggling with attention and/or executive function.

Practice and Application Activities to Consider

Mix It Up	*Who's Got It*	*"Read" It*	*In a Word*
Students scramble several (4–8) magnet letters or tiles. Teacher says a letter sound. Student selects the letter and repeats the sound four times.	Each student gets one letter. Teacher says a sound. The child with this letter shows it. Everyone says the name and sound four times.	Students find a target letter in a Big Book, letter book, or other large-print passage. When they find the letter, they say the sound ("reading" the sound).	Teacher says a word and children select the letter that represents the first, final, or medial sound. Students repeat the sound.

Based on Roberts et al., 2019; Jones et al., 2013

Prompt. Prompt children after every practice or application opportunity to ensure they all get to the correct response.

- If a student can't articulate a letter's sound, try: "*B* spells /b/. Say /b/ [point to the letter]." Have the student say /b/ four more times while pointing to the letter.
- If a student can't select a letter based on its sound, try: "That is an *o* /o/. *A* /a/ looks similar, but it has a line beside the circle. Say /a/ [point to the letter]."

Progress Monitoring and Moving On

Children's alphabet knowledge should improve with repetition and practice. Use the review portion of this lesson to assess children's progress informally. Be sure to note the letters children continue to struggle with and circle back to them in future lessons. Sometimes, children may need an extraordinary amount of practice and support, and they may require additional services. Continue to focus on alphabet knowledge until children reach mastery; if they don't know *g* spells /g/ on Tuesday, they will not miraculously know it on Wednesday, without deliberate instruction and practice.

However, that does not mean we should withhold books from kids! Children do not need to have mastered the alphabet to begin decoding. Once children are able to recognize about eight consonants and at least three vowels, start integrating decoding and encoding practice, even into your alphabet lessons.

Changing the Rigor	Total Number of Letters	Practice vs. Application	Moving to Decoding
START HERE	Focus on about four letters to start.	Focus on practice activities.	Identify letters in words (and saying sounds).
INCREASE THE RIGOR	Use eight or more letters along with the target letter.	Include at least one application activity per lesson.	Model decoding with a target letter sound.

4.2 How to Support Discriminating and Articulating Phonemes

Purpose: To help children identify and articulate phonemes with explicit instruction in articulation.*

Problem This Routine Solves

There is no denying the importance of phonemic awareness, or the ability to hear, isolate, and say the smallest unit in our language: the phoneme. For many children, this isn't too difficult. But, for some children, particularly children learning English, accurately distinguishing similar phonemes and/or articulating phonemes may get in the way of their progress (Roberts, 2005).

Does this sound familiar?

Children who can't discriminate and/or articulate sounds may:

- Consistently mix up similar sounds: Name the first sound in *map*? /n/.
- Add schwa to sounds: /kuh/ instead of /k/.
- Show a language-specific difficulty. A student who speaks Spanish may find it difficult to say the /j/ sound, a new phoneme for most Spanish speakers.
- Have a dialect difference. For example, a student who speaks African American English likely drops the final /d/ or changes it to /t/ in some words. To learn about teaching students with dialect differences, read the work of Brandy Gatlin-Nash, Lakeisha Johnson, Ryan Lee-James, and Julie Washington.

What the Research Says

Several studies have investigated the impact of articulation instruction on phonemic awareness. They find that including articulation instruction, along with phonemic awareness practice with letters, can improve children's segmenting and decoding skills (Becker & Sylvan, 2021; Boyer & Ehri, 2011; Castiglioni-Spalten & Ehri, 2003). They also find pairing articulation instruction with alphabet learning might benefit children, especially children learning English (Roberts et al., 2019; Novelli et al., 2024).

Effective articulation instruction includes teaching children how to form phonemes with descriptions of how to produce the sound (e.g., mouth formation, tongue placement, voice on or off) and examples (watching a teacher's mouth and looking at pictures). Children can also benefit from watching their own mouths form phonemes in mirrors.

*The examples in this chapter are in Standard American English.

A Note About Multilingual Learners

To best support children in discriminating and articulating phonemes, start with their home language. When children are trying to articulate a phoneme in English that does not exist in their home language, they may need additional support. But you can only offer that support if you know a little bit about their home language. Below are some examples of differences between English, Spanish, and Arabic. Spanish and Arabic are the two most common languages spoken at home by children identified as being English learners.

Examples of English phonemes that may pose a challenge for Spanish speakers:

- /v/ and /b/ are typically not distinguishable in Spanish.
- /z/ does not exist in Spanish; it might be replaced with the /s/ sound.
- /j/ does not exist in Spanish; it might be replaced with /d/ or /ch/.

Examples of English phonemes that may pose a challenge for Arabic speakers:

- /p/ does not exist in Arabic; it might be replaced with /b/.
- /v/ does not exist in Arabic; it might be replaced with /f/.
- Modern Standard Arabic does not have /g/, but some dialects do include /g/.

Please note these are not comprehensive lists. I highly encourage you to learn more about the languages spoken in your classroom. Some states, such as Colorado, and professional organizations, such as the American Speech-Language-Hearing Association, have great resources for learning about and comparing across languages.

Routine (About 10 minutes)

Review. Review sound-spelling correspondences you've taught by showing a letter and the corresponding articulation card and asking children to say its sound.

Teach. Use the same explicit, systematic language that you use in whole-class alphabet instruction, and focus on articulation of individual phonemes. "This is *J* /j/ [show the letter]. Watch my mouth [point to your mouth]: /j/, /j/ [show articulation card]. This is a mouth making the /j/ sound. Say /j/ while you watch your mouth in the mirror."

Materials

- Sound boxes (for more on sound boxes, see Routine 4.4)
- Articulation cards
- Hand mirrors
- Letter tiles or magnets
- For Picture This!: Pictures representing each word students will work with across the lesson (may be particularly helpful for English learners)

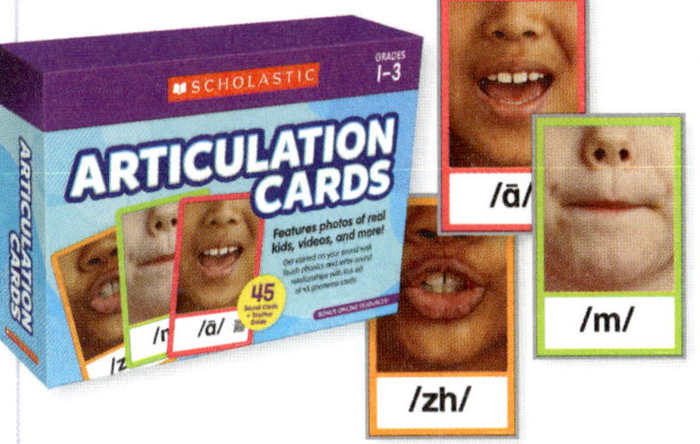

Draw children's attention to similar sounds: "When I make the sound /j/ in *jump*, my voice is on. But when I make the sound /ch/ in *champ*, my voice is off. You try."

Then model how to discriminate the sounds in words. "We can listen for sounds in words and tell the sounds. Watch me find the first sound in a word. I'll say a word and watch my mouth in the mirror: *jam*. *Jam*. Now, I'll focus on the first sound: /j/ *aaam*, /j/. The first sound was /j/. I'll select the picture that matches my mouth [show articulation card] and put it in the first box. *Jam* starts with /j/. Last, I can select the letter that spells /j/, *j*."

Practice and Apply. Have children practice isolating the target phoneme in words. After they isolate each phoneme, give them the chance to apply what they've learned by selecting the corresponding articulation card and letter. Be sure to let them practice previously learned phonemes, too.

For students who are learning English, consider showing a picture of the word, giving a student-friendly definition of it, or giving an example of a sentence containing it to make a direct connection to vocabulary learning.

Practice Activities to Consider		
Picture This!	***Whose Mouth Is It Anyway?***	***Sam Says***
Show a picture of a word with the target phoneme. Have students identify the picture and say the word. Correct whole-word pronunciation if needed. Then have students watch their mouths in the mirror as they say the word and segment the sound. Have them select the corresponding articulation card and then the corresponding letter.	Show three articulation cards. Point to each and say the sound. Have students repeat the sounds. Next, show three letters and have students match each letter to one articulation card/sound. Then say a word that starts with one of the three sounds. Have them repeat the word, isolate the first sound, and point to the picture showing the initial sound.	Start with an alliterative sentence stem (e.g., "Sam says" or "Tim tells"). Have students identify the first sound and letter (put letter in sound box). Ask, "Does Sam say it?" Fill in the blank with words that do and do not alliterate ("Sam says *hello*" = no. "Sam says *surprise*" = yes). Have students isolate the first sound, show the letter, and tell if Sam says it.

Based on Becker & Sylvan, 2021; Cárdenas-Hagan, 2020; Castiglioni-Spalten & Ehri, 2003

Prompt. Help students accurately articulate each phoneme by prompting them along these lines.

- If a student says a similar sound, try giving specific comparison information: "When we say /v/, our voice is on. When we say /f/, our voice is off."
- If a student says the wrong sound, try modeling again: "Watch me. *Sag*, /g/. Make your mouth look like mine."

Progress Monitoring and Moving On

The goal of phonemic discrimination and articulation is for children to use those skills to decode and encode. The goal is not to ensure that all children speak exactly the same way or pronounce every phoneme the same way. Continue to use the tools in this chapter, even as children begin reading and spelling words, to support articulation. Doing that will strengthen their reading and writing.

Changing the Rigor	Phonemes	Sound Position to Isolate	Isolation to Segmentation	Manipulatives
START HERE	Focus on one challenging phoneme at a time.	Initial sound	Isolate one sound in a word.	Mirrors and articulation cards
INCREASE THE RIGOR	Discriminate and articulate several challenging phonemes.	Final sound and then medial sound	Segment two or three sounds in a word (see Routine 4.4!).	No manipulatives (or counters/letters)

4.3 How to Support Blending Three Sounds

Purpose: To help children blend three sounds by engaging them in successive blending.

Problem This Routine Solves

Most children learn to decode consonant-vowel-consonant (CVC) words by sounding out each letter one at a time and then blending the three sounds together to say the word. But children who struggle to blend individual sounds in sequence may benefit from a different approach called successive blending, which helps them bundle the first two sounds and then blend this "bundle" with the final sound more smoothly (Beck & Beck, 2013).

Does this sound familiar?

Children who can't blend three sounds may:

- Blend just the rime: /k/ /a/ /t/, *at*?
- Never blend the sounds: /k/ /a/ /t/ ... /k/ /a/ /t/ ... /k/ /a/ /t/
- Blend using the wrong initial sound: /k/ /a/ /t/, *tat*
- Add schwa sounds while blending: /kuh/ /a/ /tuh/ ... *caatuh*?

What the Research Says

By bundling the initial consonant sound with the medial vowel sound, children may blend sounds more easily in three key ways:

- Children will eliminate the confusing schwa sound added to stop sounds (*buh* instead of /b/) by bundling initial stop sounds with medial vowels.
- Children can hold the medial vowel sound, a continuous sound, into the final sound, without breaking the speech stream. Multiple studies demonstrate that teaching children to avoid breaking the speech stream while blending and segmenting leads to superior skills (Constable, 2010; Gonzalez-Frey & Ehri, 2021; Hassler et al., 2025).
- Children blend phonemes from left to right, which is most effective. Sargiani and his colleagues (2022) found that teaching children to blend consonant-vowel units (not words,

Successive blending: bundling sounds to blend across a word.

Typical phoneme-by-phoneme blending: /c/ /a/ /t/, *cat*

Successive blending: /c/ /c/ /a/, *ca* /caaaaa/ /t/, *cat*

just word parts) supported phonemic awareness, decoding, and spelling. Blending consonant-vowel units and then adding the final consonant keeps children focused on blending individual phonemes from left to right, rather than word family-focused blending (*mat*: /at/ /m/ /at/, *mat*), which is a less effective approach at this phase of development (Al Otaiba et al., 2019).

In this blending lesson, you'll notice that children do actually use letters. Combining phonemic awareness with letters is the best way to improve skills (Stalega et al., 2024).

Routine (About 7 minutes)

Review. Review target letter-sound correspondences by showing a letter and having children say its sound. Doing that will make practice and application of successive blending proceed more smoothly.

Teach. To teach successive blending, use explicit language such as, "To blend the sounds of a word, I can bundle them. The word is *sat*. I can say the first sound /s/. Then hold it and run into the second sound /ssssa/. And now hold the second sound into the third /saaaaaat/. Watch again. The word is *mat*: /m/ /mmma/ /maaaaat/." Model successive blending with two to three more words.

Practice and Apply. Have students practice successive blending orally by giving them a word and having them move counters across word boxes. Then have them apply this to the same word, using letters. Start with two-sound words (*at*, *see*) or word parts (*mi*, *sa*).

- Say the segmented word or word part: "/m/.../a/."
- Have students say the initial sound while moving their counter into the first box. Then say the initial sound and medial sound together as students move the counter into the second box, and, from there, say the word or word part: "/m/ ... /m/ /a/, *ma*."
- Put the letters in the word boxes. Repeat the process with the same word or word part, but with the letters visible.

Materials

- Word boxes with counters
- Magnetic letters, letter tiles, or written word list
- 5–10 letter-sound correspondences to focus on per lesson—words should include only those correspondences (aim for 10–20 words per lesson)
  - Example sound-spelling list: *a, i, m, s, f, d, t, p, n*
  - Example word list: *mid, man, miss, sad, sim, Sam, nap, fit, fat, fan, fad, fin, fam, Tim, pin, pad, did, dip, dad, dim*

For children who need to solidify alphabet knowledge, select mostly known letters for lessons targeting blending.

For some students, practicing this skill with three or more sounds orally may be confusing. Though it may seem counterintuitive, you might skip oral practice and move directly into application with letters, once children get the basic principle of successive blending.

Prompt. Ensure your prompting focuses on children saying every sound in the word accurately.

- If a student is pausing between each sound, try: "When we're saying the sounds, we're going to keep our motor running and run into the last sound in the word. Watch me: *mmmmmmmmaaaaat*!"
- If a student is adding or changing a sound, try this: "Say the word with me and watch my mouth. Feel how your mouth makes the first sound, /b/. Now, try again and make sure you feel that sound."

Progress Monitoring and Moving On

Children's blending skills should improve quickly with differentiated instruction and practice in small groups. Track how many words children correctly blend during each small-group lesson. When children consistently blend five to seven words correctly in a row, increase the rigor (based on Gonzalez-Frey & Ehri's 2021 protocol). Once children consistently blend three sounds, including stop sounds (either by successive blending or phoneme-by-phoneme blending), move them into more decoding-focused experiences.

Changing the Rigor	Type of Phonemes to Blend	Total Number of Phonemes	Number of Phonemes to Blend per Word or Word Part
START HERE	Use only continuous consonant sounds in the initial position (*map, sag*).	About eight phonemes (and letters!)	Two sounds (*at, it, sa, mo*)
INCREASE THE RIGOR	Include stop consonant sounds (*bat, cup*).	All known phonemes	Three sounds (*cap, mom, got*)

4.4 How to Support Segmenting Three Sounds

Purpose: To provide students with more targeted practice in segmenting three sounds using counters and letters.

Problem This Routine Solves

Segmenting is one of the strongest early predictors of reading success (Hatcher & Hulme, 1999). Children cannot spell if they cannot segment sounds. Some children will master segmenting with brief, whole-class instruction (Rice et al., 2022). Other children need more practice to solidify their skills, and manipulatives often help. Targeted, supported practice with word boxes is one evidence-based way to improve phoneme segmenting and, over time, word reading and spelling.

Does this sound familiar?

Children who can't segment may:

- Just say the first sound in a word rather than all sounds.
- Attempt to segment *cat* as /c/ /at/ and call it two sounds (and may point to two boxes if using word and sound boxes).
- Skip the vowel sound when segmenting (*mat*, /m/ /t/).
- Skip sounds when spelling (*mat* spelled *mt*).
- Capture all sounds, but incorrectly (*mat* spelled *m-i-t* or *n-a-t*). These students may need more support in discriminating sounds (4.2) or matching letter-sound correspondences (4.1).

What the Research Says

Explicitly teaching children to segment words improves reading, even over time. In one study, kindergartners who were taught to segment had significantly higher reading scores in first grade than their peers (Ball & Blachman, 1991). Just like blending practice, segmenting practice is best when it includes letters (Erbeli et al., 2024; Stalega et al., 2024).

Word boxes are powerful tools to teach segmenting to beginning readers (Joseph, 2002). When children need this support, practicing with word boxes can improve phonemic awareness, decoding, and spelling from pre-K to fifth grade (Aspiranti et al., 2024; Ross & Joseph, 2019). The best way to practice with word boxes is through three phases: saying the sounds, adding letter tiles or magnets, and spelling the word on handwriting lines (Ross & Joseph, 2019).

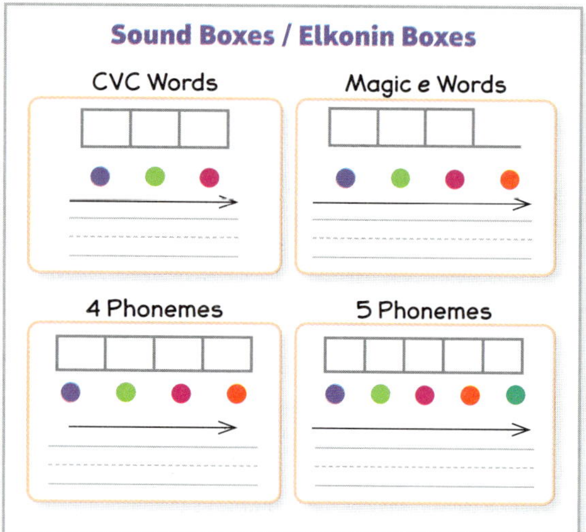

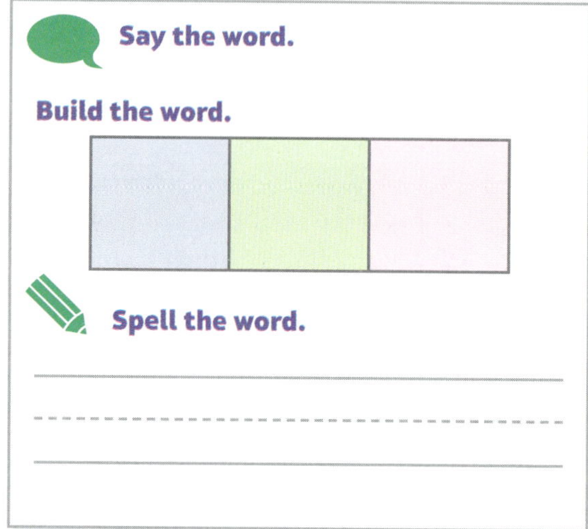

Materials

- Word boxes with counters
- Magnetic letters or letter tiles (select 5–10 known sound-spelling correspondences to focus on per lesson; words should only include these spellings; aim for 10–20 words per lesson)
- Whiteboards for children to draw their own boxes and handwrite
- Word boxes with handwriting lines

Routine (About 7 minutes)

Review. Review target letter-sound correspondences by showing a letter and having children say its sound so children are ready to segment.

Teach. Show students a word and sound boxes and say, "We can listen for and say all the sounds in a word. This helps us to become awesome spellers! Watch me. I'll say a word: *sap*. Next, I'll say it slowly, counting all the sounds on my boxes: *ssssaaaaap* [point to three boxes]. Then I can put a counter into each box for each sound" [slide a counter into each box as you speak].

To add letters: "Now, I'll look at my letters and select a letter for each sound [point to the first counter and then push up the correct letter]: /s/ *s*, /a/ *a*, /p/ *p*, *sap*! Last, I can spell the word on the lines: *ssssaaaap* [handwrite the word on the lines]. *Sap*."

Practice and Apply. Have children segment sounds using the word boxes. For practice, focus on sounds only. For application, add in letters. In most cases, the best procedure is this basic procedure (see Word Box It below).

- Repeat the word.
- Say the word slowly and count the sounds in the word [touching boxes].
- Say each sound and push one chip into each box.
- Say each sound and push letter(s) into each box.
- Write the word beneath the boxes.
- Read the whole word to check.

Practice Activities		Application Activities	
Mouth to Sound	***Sounds in a Word***	***Word Box It***	***How Many Sounds?***
*Use after explicit instruction in articulation cards. See Routine 4.2. Say a word. Have students repeat the word and segment the word counting sounds. Then have them put articulation cards in boxes for each sound.	Show a picture of a word. Have students identify the picture and say the word. Correct whole-word pronunciation if needed. Have students repeat the word and segment the word counting sounds. Then have them put counters into each box, saying each sound.	Say a word and have students repeat it. Then follow the three phases: 1) have them move a chip into each box; 2) have them insert letters for each sound; 3) have them spell the word on lines.	Say a word and have students repeat it. Then have them count the sounds in the word and draw a box for each sound. Then follow the three phases: 1) have them move a chip into each box; 2) have them insert letters for each sound; 3) have them spell the word on lines.

Based on Aspiranti et al., 2024; Castiglioni-Spalten & Ehri, 2003; Ross & Joseph, 2019

Prompt. Prompt children to accurately segment sounds. Be sure they capture the correct number of sounds, and, if you have chosen words with letter pairs that make a single sound (such as *ch*, *sh*, *ea*, *ow*), make sure students put both letters in one box.

- If a student is not able to say every sound: "Say the word slowly with me. Watch my mouth move three times: /m/ /a/ /t/. Count each sound with me: three sounds."
- If a student is not putting a counter into each box: "We put one counter in one box for one sound. How many sounds did our word have? Point to the counters and say the sounds. What are you missing?"
- If a student is not representing a sound with the correct letter: "The word is *mat* [point to wrong letter]. What sound do we need first?"

Progress Monitoring and Moving On

This might surprise you, but children's skills can improve quickly when they practice with word boxes (Larabee et al., 2014). You may see improvement in just a few short lessons. With consistent practice, children may improve their segmenting in a matter of weeks or even days. Keep track of how many words children segment correctly per lesson; once they are segmenting with over 90 percent accuracy, move on to more decoding and encoding experiences. If children continue to seem stuck in phoneme segmentation after several weeks, consider assessing phoneme discrimination and alphabet knowledge to ensure they don't need additional support.

Changing the Rigor	Counting Boxes	Supporting English Learners	Including Letters
☆ START HERE	Give children word/sound boxes with the exact number of sounds. (Tip: You might start with two-sound words.)	Use articulation cards and connect back to articulation instruction.	Brief, sounds-only practice with the counters
INCREASE THE RIGOR	Give children a blank whiteboard and have them draw boxes or lines.	Typical manipulatives (counters, letters)	Add letter tiles. Then have children handwrite words.

4.5 How to Support Forming Letters Legibly

Purpose: To provide children with targeted practice in forming letters.

Problem This Routine Solves

To become proficient writers and spellers, children must be able to form letters. Take the student-written piece in the photo below. Did this kindergartner spell *sent*? Or *sebt*? Or *seht*? It is impossible to know for sure unless we ask him, which, unfortunately, negates the goal of writing: communicating ideas. Though most phonics curricula include instruction in letter formation, and some teachers also use additional handwriting materials, research consistently finds children receive less handwriting instruction than experts recommend (McCarroll & Fletcher, 2017; Sharp & Brown, 2015). When handwriting is poor enough to delay writing development and/or to interfere with encoding practice, children need more explicit instruction, practice, and feedback.

Does this sound familiar?

Children who don't have legible enough handwriting may:

- Resist any type of writing.
- Demonstrate proficient early spelling using letter tiles or magnets, but not paper and pencil.
- Be able to identify letters and their sounds, but not be able to form letters.
- Often reverse letters when writing.

What the Research Says

Handwriting may not be the most exciting topic. It may not even seem useful in the era of smartphones, computers, and tablets. But early handwriting can predict children's spelling outcomes and is highly related to writing quality (Pritchard et al., 2021; Santangelo & Graham, 2016). Much like effortless decoding frees up cognitive resources for comprehension, effortless handwriting enables children to devote more cognitive resources to composing and other writing processes (Graham, 1999).

Explicit handwriting instruction, particularly individualized instruction, combined with daily practice improves both the legibility and quality of students' writing (Santangelo & Graham, 2016). Several instructional elements make handwriting instruction more impactful, including lined paper and letter-formation arrows (Berninger et al., 2006); practice tracing, copying, and writing from memory (Mathwin et al., 2022); and immediate feedback (López-Escribano et al., 2022). Additionally, explicit, multisensory instruction in handwriting may minimize letter reversals (e.g., *dat* vs. *bat*) (Berninger et al., 2006).

Learning and practicing letter formation may also build alphabet knowledge, particularly for English learners (Roberts, 2021). The following routine aims to improve children's letter-sound knowledge, along with handwriting (Mathwin et al., 2022).

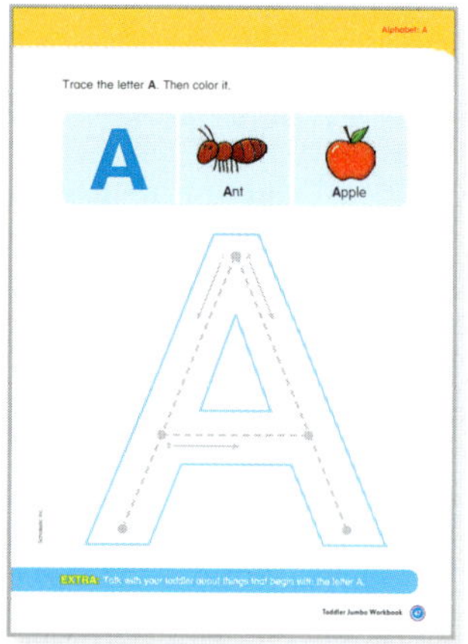

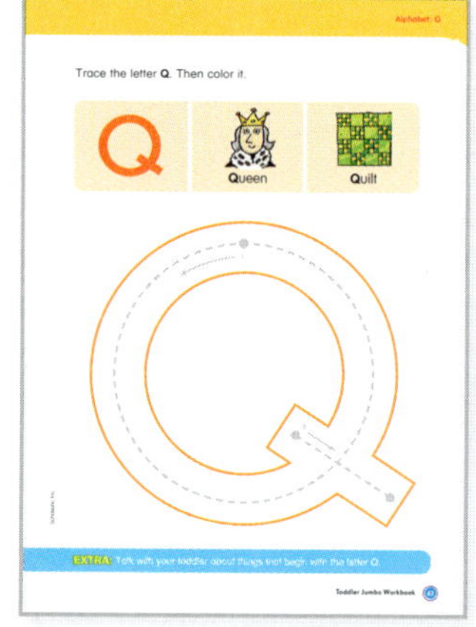

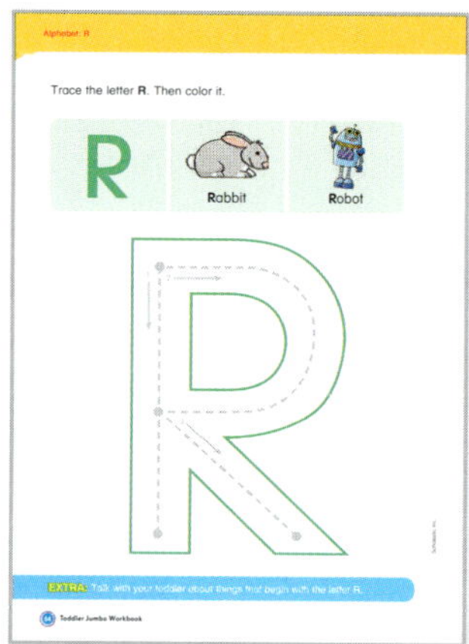

letter stroke cards

Materials

- Paper for tracing and writing (must have lines and letter strokes—I recommend downloading from the Iowa Reading Research Center's free tool, Literacy LIFTER)
- Letter stroke cards

Routine (Less than 5 minutes)

Review. Have children practice forming letters they've learned. Specifically, select about five letters for children to form about five times each.

Teach. To teach a new letter formation, tell the strokes (such as a line down) and order: "To form the lowercase *b* /b/, start at the top, make a straight line all the way down, go to the middle, and bump around: *b* /b/ [model forming the letter]."

Practice and Apply. Have children practice forming the target letter by tracing letter strokes at least eight times. Then, on blank lined paper, have children practice the letter again at least eight times. As they form the letter, prompt them to say the sound. After each attempt at forming the letter, have children compare their version to the model and notice what they need to fix. Eventually, you may have children practice writing words containing the target letter on lined paper.

Prompt. When you devote even a tiny bit of time to targeted small-group instruction in letter formation and handwriting, it gives you a chance to give children clear, precise direction. These prompts are based on research by Mathwin and colleagues (2022).

- If a student can't form the letter after you cover it: "Can you picture the letter *d* in your mind? Try to see it and then form it."
- If a student forms the letter incorrectly: "Did you form a *d*? Check our letter *d* card to see why yours is not the correct shape."
- If a student places the letter incorrectly: "Have you followed the rules of where the letter should sit on the lines?"

Progress Monitoring and Moving On

Handwriting skills improve with daily, repeated practice over time. In some studies, children's handwriting improves in as little as five hours of instruction over the year. Handwriting is important. That said, try not to go overboard. A student with perfect handwriting who can't decode or encode is still not a reader or a writer. I recommend using no more than five minutes up to five times a week per group for handwriting. To ensure children get enough practice, start with your explicit whole-class instruction and give students handwriting practice worksheets (such as Literacy LIFTER). For children who are struggling, add explicit instruction and supported practice in small groups.

Changing the Rigor	Tracing, Copying, Remembering	Practice vs. Application
START HERE	Focus on tracing letters.	Focus on the target letter.
INCREASE THE RIGOR	Focus on having children form letters from memory.	Add one to three opportunities to write a whole word, including the target letter and previously practiced letters.

In Closing, Remember This Swap

Less "wait and see" → More targeted practice right away for alphabet knowledge and phonemic awareness.

When students are building skills in the alphabet and in phonemic awareness, it is far more important to intervene early than to second-guess if a student demonstrates "enough" of a need. Research shows that children with specific needs in phonemic awareness will benefit from supplemental instruction, no matter their age; however, this instruction is the most impactful when children are in kindergarten and first grade (Rehfeld et al., 2022; Rice et al.,

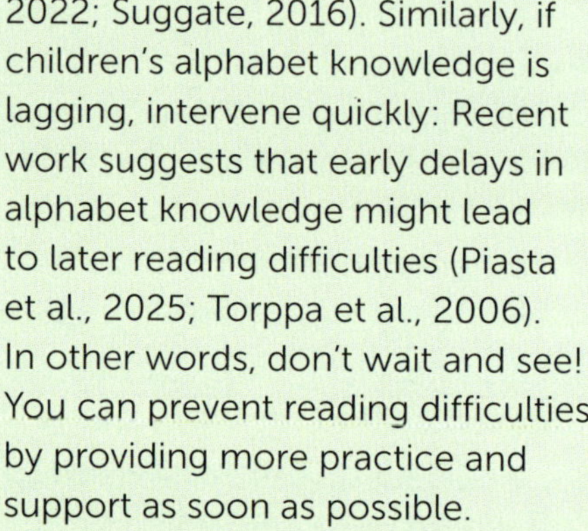

2022; Suggate, 2016). Similarly, if children's alphabet knowledge is lagging, intervene quickly: Recent work suggests that early delays in alphabet knowledge might lead to later reading difficulties (Piasta et al., 2025; Torppa et al., 2006). In other words, don't wait and see! You can prevent reading difficulties by providing more practice and support as soon as possible.

The best way to provide this supportive practice is with small-group instruction. The routines in this chapter all focus on the core purpose of small-group instruction: getting children the supported, targeted practice they need to continue to grow as readers. If you aren't sure where to start, begin with one skill and one routine. For example, does every student in your class know the alphabet? Try focusing on using Routine 4.1, which should feel familiar if you teach the alphabet during whole-class instruction, to accelerate learning and get kids ready to decode.

CHAPTER 5

Developing Decoding Skills

Children who are developing decoding skills are rapidly becoming word readers. They use knowledge about sound-spelling correspondences and phonemic awareness to decode and encode words (Ehri, 2014). Through repeated, supported practice and application in texts, children decode increasingly complex words. Decoding skills are truly the backbone of proficient readers because they are essential for orthographic mapping, or connecting a word's spelling to its pronunciation and its meaning to store in long-term memory and recognize on sight (Ehri, 2017). Becoming a decoder may feel like magic, but it is actually the result of lots of hard work and practice. For more on why decoding is important, check out Chapter 2 in my book *Reading Above the Fray*.

But decoding takes a lot of cognitive energy. When children are decoding most words they encounter in text, they do not have much energy left to engage in making meaning. The goal of instruction in decoding is to move children efficiently toward recognizing many words automatically, which requires lots of practice in:

- Matching spellings and sounds, including less frequent ones.
- Decoding words in isolation and in texts.
- Encoding words in isolation and in texts.

The routines in this chapter give children the opportunity to practice in each of those skills.

What Do Children Need to Practice?

To become strong decoders, children must practice:

- Decoding words in isolation and in meaningful contexts. This practice leads to orthographic mapping, which enables students to connect a word's spelling to its pronunciation and meaning (Routines 5.1 and 5.2). For more on orthographic mapping, check out Molly Ness and Katie Pace Miles's book *Making Words Stick*.
- Connecting sounds and spellings, particularly challenging sounds and spellings, to decode and encode words. In particular, children can get stuck on vowel sounds. Practice and instruction that supports flexibility in vowel knowledge can help (Routine 5.3).
- Decoding and encoding words with three or more sounds. Children can get stuck moving beyond basic consonant-vowel-consonant (CVC) words, even with enough sound-spelling knowledge and adequate phonemic awareness. Emphasizing high-impact encoding practice can help (Routine 5.4).
- Decoding high-frequency words. Some children can struggle connecting irregular sound-spellings to certain high-frequency words. Lots of repeated practice and application can help (Routine 5.5).

Much like building alphabet knowledge and phonemic awareness, developing decoding skills requires feedback, as well as practice. All children developing decoding skills need at least some instruction in smaller groups to receive direct, immediate input to ensure they are acquiring critical word-recognition skills.

Logistics of Small-Group Instruction to Develop Decoding Skills

The most common questions I get about developing decoding and encoding skills in small groups include:

- In what grades are children most likely to be developing decoding and encoding skills?
- How should I group students?
- What materials do I need?
- Where do I find good decodable texts?
- How often should students read decodables?
- What should children do when they aren't in small groups?

In what grades are children most likely to be developing decoding and encoding skills?

Children in the second half of kindergarten, first grade, and the beginning of second grade are most likely to be developing these skills. Once children can recognize some single-syllable words automatically, such as words with long-vowel patterns, they are ready for more challenges with multisyllabic words.

How should I group students?

There are a few ways to group students developing decoding skills. Here are two suggestions.

Option 1: Assess students using a decoding inventory, such as the Informal Decoding Inventory (see Chapter 2), to place children along a sequence of decoding skills. Group students based on where they fall along the sequence, as in this example.

CVC words	Consonant Blends and Digraphs	CVC-*e*
Sophie, Jack, Miles	Amelia, David, Charlie, Amber	Paulie, Kaden, Mai, Naeem

Option 2: Assess students with a weekly check (see Chapter 2). Group students based on their errors, which may include previously learned phonics skills or the skill you taught that week. You may also group students based on spelling high-frequency words or previously learned words.

Weekly check after teaching *ch* and *sh*: *chin, dash, shut, rich, I wish to get on a ship.*			
0–2 words correct	**3–4 words correct**	**5–6 words correct**	**3–5 high-frequency words incorrect**
Zara, Coco, Reece	Xavier, Mila, Eleanor	Fatima, Luis, Olivia	Olivia, Xavier, Zara, Coco
Target the previous skill, CVC word knowledge, with Routine 5.4	Target *ch* and *sh* in texts with Routine 5.1	Target *ch* and *sh* in knowledge-connected texts with Routine 5.2	Target high-frequency words with Routine 5.5

What materials do I need?

Practice in decoding and encoding skills does not require fancy materials. At a minimum, you'll need decodable texts, word lists, and some mini whiteboards with handwriting lines. That's it!

To come up with word lists, use your phonics program and scope and sequence. At least half of each list should include the lesson's target sound-spelling correspondences. The rest of it should include previously learned content. You can also include words straight out of the decodable text—repetition is great for fueling orthographic mapping!

If you want to add variety in children's practice, make a few more materials available to them. You'll notice I suggest these items for the routines on pages 79 to 96.

- Words printed on individual cards
- Word boxes
- Vowel cards or chart
- Dice
- Magnetic letters
- Pictures of key vocabulary words

Where do I find good decodable texts?

First, let's define "good" decodables. Good decodables give children the chance to decode lots of words with sound-spelling correspondences they need to practice. Good decodables make sense and are interesting to students. Good decodables use natural language and syntax.

The best approach is to match decodable texts directly to student needs. For example, though your first graders may be learning consonant digraphs in whole-class instruction, some of them may still be solidifying CVC decoding and will likely benefit more from a text with a high proportion of CVC words, along with known high-frequency words. The easiest way to match skills to texts is using the UFLI Foundations Toolbox, which lists texts from more than 60 companies aligned to specific skills along its scope and sequence, including Scholastic's Short Reads Decodables and Read to Know Text Sets. No matter what phonics scope and sequence you use, this toolbox is a great starting point for finding texts that match specific skills.

How often should students read decodables?

There's no perfect answer to this question. Ideally, all children developing decoding skills have the opportunity to read decodable texts every day. After teaching a new skill, you should give them a chance to read at least one decodable in a small group (to receive feedback). Have children continue to read decodables independently or with partners, particularly if children have stronger skills.

What should children do when they aren't in small groups?

Much like children developing alphabet knowledge and phonemic awareness, children developing decoding skills can—and should—practice some skills on their own. Remember, children with weaker skills are less likely to benefit from lots of independent practice, so focus on partner activities and tech-supported activities.

Games: After playing a game during small-group instruction, students can continue playing it in pairs. Roll and Read is a good choice! I once watched groups of first graders in Lindsay Kemeny's class play it independently and joyfully for 20 minutes.

Materials needed

- Roll and Read sheet (see the one at right for an example)
- Highlighters, crayons, or markers
- A die

Partner A: Rolls the die, picks a word in the corresponding column, reads it, highlights it.

Partner B: Reads the word and agrees or disagrees with Partner A's decoding.

Then partners switch roles.

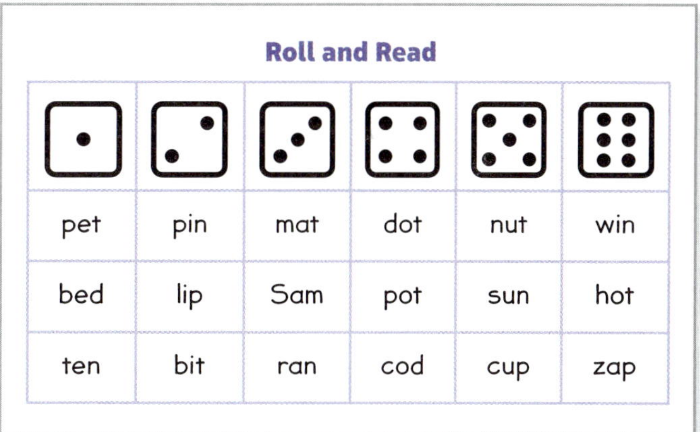

Roll and Read

pet	pin	mat	dot	nut	win
bed	lip	Sam	pot	sun	hot
ten	bit	ran	cod	cup	zap

Tech Tools. The best tech tools for developing decoders connect to instruction. In other words, if students are practicing words with silent *e* in small-group instruction, technology will help them most by giving them practice decoding and encoding words with silent *e* (Verhoeven et al., 2020). Many apps provide that type of practice. A few research-based options for decoding practice include Lexia, English Islands, and Magpie Literacy.

Partner Reading. Have students read and reread a decodable text and then retell it to one another when they're finished. Pair students with stronger and weaker decoding skills to ensure accuracy. (Before pairing students, teach them how to be good partners in small groups—specifically how to take turns, pause together to check for understanding, and give polite, helpful feedback when a partner reads a word incorrectly.)

Ebooks With Audio. Students may enjoy listening to content-connected ebooks and benefit from those with supportive features, such as highlighting the words as they are read and prompting for challenging words (e.g., a student touches a word to hear it read aloud). Be aware, though, that it is not clear if ebook reading is any more beneficial than traditional reading (Karemaker et al., 2017), and that some features (such as video elements) that claim to be supportive are not, and may in fact distract students from the words.

Step-by-Step Routines for Developing Decoding Skills

Developing decoding skills requires many encounters with words in isolated practice and in texts. The routines that follow offer a mix of both. All students developing word recognition skills need the chance to decode texts with support. Use Routines 5.1 and 5.2 for all students to provide that practice. Use the remaining routines to give students more explicit instruction, practice, application, and feedback when they need it.

➔ **Go here to see a video demonstration of a Chapter 5 routine in action.**

➔ **Go here for downloadable resources for these Chapter 5 routines.**

5.1 How to Teach Basic Decoding in Context

Purpose: To support children in decoding by providing immediate, direct feedback while reading decodable texts.

Problem This Routine Solves

The goal of decoding instruction is to enable children to read whole texts. Though some isolated word work is essential, children cannot become readers by decoding individual words only (van Bergen et al., 2021). Simply put, developing decoders need to decode words in context.

Does this sound familiar?

Children who will benefit from decodable texts may:

- Accurately decode words in isolation, but struggle to decode words in texts.
- Read some words automatically, but are slow to decode recently learned sound-spelling patterns.
- Decode most words they encounter (in isolation or in books).

What the Research Says

Decodable texts are texts that children can read, assuming they have the phonics skills to do so. They include a high proportion of known decodable words (words with sound-spelling correspondences that have been taught and learned) and known high-frequency words. When reading decodable texts, children are more likely to be accurate, rely less on their teacher, and apply decoding skills to words that may be unfamiliar (Mesmer, 2005). Reading decodable texts supports word recognition development more than other types of texts, such as leveled texts (Murphy Odo, 2024).

Selecting decodable texts. When selecting decodable texts for small-group instruction, consider the specific skills each group of students needs to practice. While one approach is to use your phonics scope and sequence, a better approach is to match texts directly to student needs. For example, though your first graders may be learning consonant digraphs, if some of them are still solidifying CVC words, they will likely benefit more from a text with a high proportion of CVC words, along with high-frequency words they know. To support children beyond simply decoding individual words, select texts that are meaningful and interesting and contain natural language and syntax.

Giving feedback. As children acquire decoding skills, they need immediate, direct feedback. But it is impossible to give that to every student during whole-class lessons. So give it to them in small groups. Research suggests that children who receive such feedback (e.g., "Check the vowel sound again" or "In this word, *ch* spells /ch/. Try it again") have better reading outcomes (Rodgers et al., 2016).

Materials

- Decodable text matched to student skill
- Word list with about 20 words
- Additional materials based on the practice activity

Routine (About 12 minutes)

Review. Review previously taught sound-spelling correspondences by showing the spelling and having children say the sound.

Teach. For children who are keeping up with your scope and sequence: Teach the newest sound-spelling and how to decode it, using precise, explicit language: "*c* and *h* together spell the sound /ch/. When I see *ch* in words, it is often at the beginning, like *chomp*, or at the end, like *such*. I read /ch/, not /c/ /h/."

For children who are working on previously taught content: Teach the target sound-spelling based on their assessment results, using precise, explicit language.

Practice. Have children briefly practice with the sound-spelling target (each word = one practice opportunity; see below). Children need multiple opportunities to decode each word to generate an orthographic map and read the word automatically (Bowey & Muller, 2005; Nation et al., 2007; Share, 2004). By starting with this practice, children will be more prepared to decode within a text.

Practice Activities to Consider		
Hear, Say, Spell Students hear a word with the sound-spelling target. Then have them segment the word while tapping on each Elkonin box. Finally, have students spell the word.	***Decode It!*** Each student gets a list of words (about half include the target sound-spelling). Lists are varied so students decode words in different sequences. Have students whisper-decode each word two times while you give feedback.	***Partner Check*** Pair up students. Give each partner half of the words (make sure each list has some of the sound-spelling target!). Partner 1 will read a word while Partner 2 spells. Then check the word. Switch partner roles.

Based on Aspiranti et al., 2024; Joseph, 2002

Apply. Introduce the text to students. Give a reason for reading that goes beyond practicing decoding, such as "I think you'll like this book" or "This book is about rain, which can help us learn more about weather, the topic of our science unit." Then have students start reading the book in a whisper to themselves. Make sure you're positioned to be able to lean in to each student and give feedback.

After children read, ask at least one reasonable, text-dependent question ("Did you think this story was funny? Why or why not?") or a question that is connected to content learning ("What did you learn about rain?"). Though most decodable texts are not written for deep comprehension work, aim for meaning nonetheless.

Prompt. Respond when you hear decoding errors, starting with the least amount of support and gradually increasing support if needed (Duke, 2020).

- If a student makes an error, say something like, "Look at the word and all its letters."
- If a student misses or changes a sound, say something like, "Try saying each sound again."
    - Then: "What sound does that spell?" (Point to a spelling.)
    - Finally: "*ch* spells /ch/. Try the word again."
- If a student cannot decode the word after multiple attempts, say something like, "This word is [say word]. Your turn!"

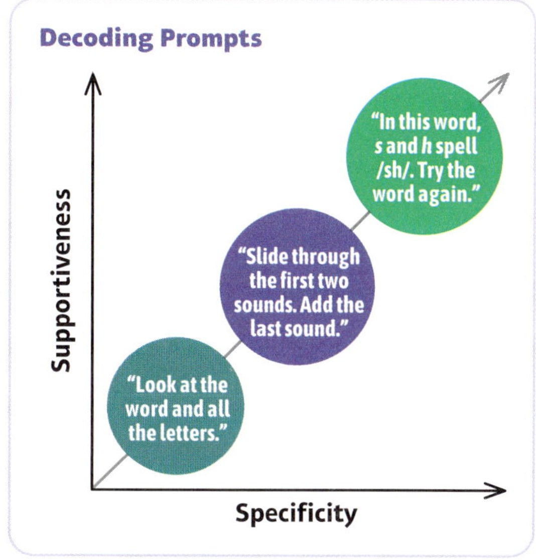

Progress Monitoring and Moving On

All developing decoders deserve the opportunity to apply their knowledge in texts and receive supportive feedback. Aim for all students to read at least one decodable text connected to each new phonics concept. For children progressing along your scope and sequence, move on to the next concept on it. For children struggling to keep up, move on to the next concept when they demonstrate accurate decoding, even if they are not doing it automatically. As students gain proficiency in basic CVC word decoding, consider increasing the rigor and variety of texts. See Routine 5.2.

Changing the Rigor	Length of Practice	Length of Supported Application	Decodable Words
START HERE	Start the lesson with about 20 practice opportunities for one sound-spelling target.	Monitor reading through the entire book.	Select texts with 90 percent or more decodable and known high-frequency words.
INCREASE THE RIGOR Increase the rigor if children are consistently demonstrating proficiency in a sound-spelling target in whole-class work.	Give three to five practice opportunities.	Listen to reading of one page and then release to read independently.	Select texts for decodability and additional elements. See Routine 5.4.

5.2 How to Teach Decoding in Knowledge-Building Contexts

Purpose: To support children in decoding by using content-connected decodable text sets.

Does this sound familiar?

Children who will benefit from content-connected decodable text sets may:

- Read some words automatically, but slow down to decode words with more recently learned sound-spelling patterns.
- Demonstrate a lack of engagement and/or motivation in typical decodable texts despite having sufficient decoding skills.
- Be able to decode/read words in decodable texts, but not be able to transfer skills into uncontrolled passages, such as oral reading fluency assessment passages.

Problem This Routine Solves

Decodable texts, by definition, offer a constrained reading experience, with language such as, "The cat sat on the mat. The rat sat on a hat. Rat sat. Cat sat. See the hat on the mat." Although essential to strengthening children's foundational skills, texts like that generally do not support their interests, motivation, knowledge, and vocabulary (Castles et al., 2018). As children move beyond the most basic phases of decoding (when they are reading CVC words with some automaticity and know some high-frequency words), they need texts that go beyond "just decodable" and support knowledge through sets of content.

What the Research Says

In recent years, some researchers have called for more "multiple criteria texts," or texts that intentionally support multiple aspects of literacy development at once (Cheatham et al., 2014; Chu & Chen, 2014; Lindsey, 2022; Vadasy et al., 2015). They consistently find that such texts can support decoding and vocabulary knowledge. In one small pilot study using content-connected decodable texts, along with knowledge-building read-aloud texts, teachers saw improvements in children's decoding, confidence, motivation, and comprehension. When books are matched to students' knowledge and interest, students are more likely to persist through challenging parts (Fulmer & Frijters, 2011).

To have the biggest possible impact on knowledge, use text sets (four to six texts on the same topic). Even young children can learn novel information from a set of texts on the same topic (Hwang et al., 2023; Kim & Zagata, 2024). Text sets should include content vocabulary, repeated across texts. This repetition may support both orthographic learning and vocabulary knowledge, and is particularly helpful for children learning English (Bowey & Muller, 2005; Teng, 2016). Introduce new vocabulary with student-friendly definitions and examples (Beck & McKeown, 2007).

Content-connected decodable texts should still be decodable. Though there is no perfect level of decodability, look for texts that are around 80 percent decodable words and known high-frequency words. The remaining 20 percent of words should ideally be those that are necessary for the text to make sense; content vocabulary words; or proper nouns.

Decodable, Knowledge-Building Texts

- **Read to Know** (Scholastic)

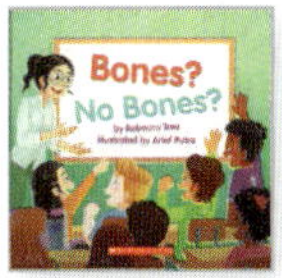

- **Geodes** (Wilson/Wit & Wisdom)
- **Article-a-Day Decodables** (ReadWorks)
- **Beyond Decodables**

Routine (About 15 minutes)

Follow the steps for Routine 5.1, How to Teach Basic Decoding in Context. Add these adaptations as necessary to also support making connections to content and vocabulary knowledge.

Materials

- Content-connected decodable text matched to student skill and knowledge target
- Word list with about 20 words
- Additional materials based on your practice (see Routine 5.1)
- Visuals for vocabulary words, if necessary

Review. Activate prior knowledge from content-area instruction, such as, "Recall that we have been reading about birds. What is one feature of birds we've learned about?"

Teach. Add a student-friendly explanation and example of a target vocabulary word in the text, such as, "A *mammal* is an animal that is warm, has fur or hair, and feeds its babies milk. Dogs are mammals." Show the word.

Practice. If vocabulary words are (1) low frequency and (2) far beyond students' current decoding skill, have students read the word after you. For the text to the right, you might pre-teach and pre-practice *kiwi* and *New Zealand*.

Apply. Introduce the book by making a clear connection to prior knowledge. After reading, have children retell what they've learned. Help them to make a connection to prior learning.

ReadWorks

What Is a Kiwi?

by Peggy Lindsey

A kiwi is a small brown bird from New Zealand. It is a bird that does not fly. Its wings are too small! It is soft and round and has no tail.

Kiwis stay in the woods. They curl up in a ball and spend the day sleeping. When it is dark, they get up and go sniffing for food. They eat bugs. They can find bugs by smelling them. Kiwis have long, thin beaks that help them

Prompt. Follow these guidelines:

- If a student misses one sound, say something like, "In this word, *e* spells /long e/. Try the word again."
- If the word includes known sounds, but more phonemes or syllables than a student can blend, say something like, "Let's break the word into parts. Decode each part. Now, put them together."
- If the word is far beyond the child's current knowledge, say something like, "This word is [say word]. Your turn!"

Avoid asking children to use context to estimate words, even words they can't decode yet. Though context can be helpful to figure out the meaning of unfamiliar words, it does not help children improve their decoding or retain words in long-term memory. Furthermore, if children are taught to rely on context to decode words, they are less likely to be able to decode words in the future, which could decrease fluency over time (Juel & Roper-Schneider, 1985; Maddox & Feng, 2013).

Progress Monitoring and Moving On

Research is inconclusive when it comes to the point at which children should move beyond decodable texts. One study found that second graders reading long vowels and multisyllabic words did not gain any benefit from independent practice in decodable texts (Cheatham et al., 2014). While advancing readers may still benefit from some opportunities to practice target sound-spelling correspondences in texts (which is certainly easier for them to do when reading decodable or multiple-criteria texts), it is critical to give them access to increasingly complex texts. When students begin automatically reading words with long-vowel patterns, start shifting to complex, grade-level texts, and monitor their decoding skills closely.

Changing the Rigor	Not-Yet-Decodable Words	Decodable Words
START HERE	Select passages with five or fewer not-yet-decodable words that are repeated.	Select texts with 80 percent or more decodable and known high-frequency words.
INCREASE THE RIGOR Increase the rigor when children are automatically reading single-syllable words with long vowels and simple multisyllabic words.	Select passages focused on target morphemes or vocabulary (Chapters 6 and 8).	Transition into grade-level texts that support multisyllabic word reading and fluency (Chapters 6 and 7).

5.3 How to Teach Typically Confusing Vowel Sounds and Spellings

Purpose: To strengthen children's flexibility in reading and spelling short vowels accurately using targeted instruction.

Problem This Routine Solves

Vowel sound-spelling correspondences can be particularly difficult for children for a variety of reasons. They may confuse similar-sounding short vowels, such as short *e* and short *i*. Vowel-sound deviations, such as the nasalized *a* (the slightly altered pronunciation of short *a* before *n* and *m* in words such as *ram* and *tan*), can add even more confusion. And that's just the short vowels! When long-vowel sounds and spellings are added to the mix, children are even more likely to experience difficulty. That's why they need instruction and practice focused on discriminating and comparing vowel sounds and spellings.

Does this sound familiar?

Children who may need support with vowels may:

- Consistently confuse *e* and *i* (or any two short vowels) in words, despite proficiency in identifying alphabet letters.
- Decode *mean* as *men* (confuse short and long sounds).
- Read *pan* as *p* /short *a*/ *n* (missing the nasalized *a*).
- Spell words (spelling *boat* *b-o-t-e*) with the wrong vowel spelling option.

What the Research Says

Two words that vary by only one sound are referred to as minimal pairs or minimal contrast pairs. During practice, we can draw children's attention to these minimal differences. Activities that have children manipulate and sort words with one sound difference can support orthographic learning of those words (Cunningham & Cunningham, 1992; Pullen & Lane, 2016; Savage et al., 2018). Accurate decoding often requires some flexibility in hearing vowel sounds. Children need to be able to adjust the pronunciation of a word, particularly its vowels, to arrive at a real, known word. That skill, which is called *set for variability*, is an essential skill to proficient reading (Elbro et al., 2012). Several studies show that a focus on this flexible reading of vowels leads to better decoding and spelling, even for young readers (Lovett et al., 2014; Savage et al., 2025).

Materials

- Vowel cards (you can also use PowerPoint slides or write the spellings on a whiteboard)
- Word list with about 10 word pairs with your target vowels (see example at right)
- Additional materials based on practice activity
- Decodable text (see Routines 5.1 and 5.2 for information about selecting texts; ensure the text has multiple opportunities with each target vowel spelling or sound)

dog	dig
jug	jog
beg	bug
dock	duck
trick	truck
mock	muck
cop	cup
cob	cub
cot	cut
knot	nut

Routine (About 12 minutes)

Review. Use vowel cards to show previously taught vowel spellings. Have children say the sound or sounds each spelling represents.

Teach. Explicitly teach children to focus on the vowel and, when necessary, adjust the vowel sound. Consider telling them to try the short sound first (because it is more frequent), and then the long sound, and finally less common sounds (Lovett et al., 2000).

Confusion About…	Example	Language
Similar sounds with different spellings	*pen* versus *pin*	Refer to Routine 4.2 for language to support children discriminating similar sounds.
Long-sound spellings	*rid* versus *ride*	"Now that we are learning about vowel teams, such as the silent *e*, we have to look all the way across a word to check our vowel sound. As you go across the word, pause and notice when you need to go back and change the vowel sound."
Vowel-sound deviations	Nasalized *a* before *n* or *m*	"The sound after a vowel can change the vowel sound. Watch my mouth when I say /short a/ versus *an*. When we see *an*, we read *an*. When we see *am*, we read *am*."
Multiple sounds for the same spelling	The sounds represented by *o* in the words *go*, *hot*, or *wolf*	"The letter *o* can spell different sounds. We can decode a word with one sound and think, 'Hmmm, is that a word?' If it isn't a word you know, you can try a different sound."

Practice. Using one of the examples below, have children practice comparing words focused on their vowel confusion.

Practice Activities to Consider

Which One?

Give students one minimal contrast pair (*rat*, *rate*). Have them read each word to themselves. Then say one of the words and have students select the word you've said. Ask, "How do you know this word is *rat*?" After all pairs, have students sort the words by vowel sound with a partner.

Roll It, Read It

Give each student a guide for spelling real and nonsense words with three sounds, like the one below. Have one student roll for the sound-spelling in the first row, and all students write it in their Sound/Spelling Boxes (e.g., C). Repeat the process for the second and third rows (e.g., A_E and N). Then have each student decode the word (e.g., CANE). Have students identify if it is a real or nonsense word.

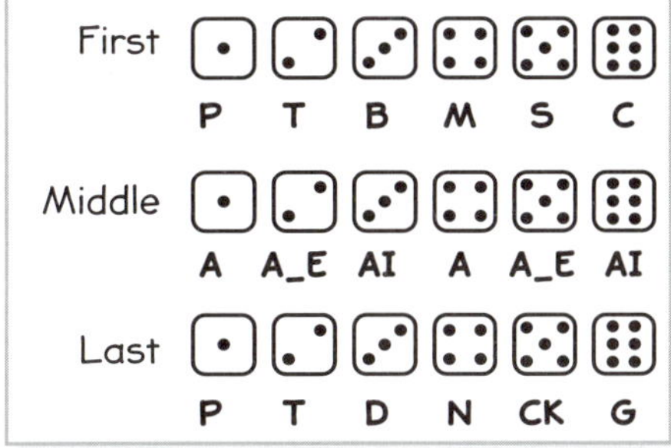

Word Building

Follow the steps for word building described in the practice section of Routine 5.4.

Based on McCandliss et al., 2003; Savage et al., 2025

Apply. After introducing the decodable text, have children whisper-read it as described in Routine 5.1. To draw children's attention even more to target vowels, have children highlight words with those vowel spellings before or after reading. Be sure to prompt children to decode and, if needed, flexibly adjust vowel sounds.

Prompt. To support children in noticing and adjusting vowel sounds, focus on prompting that draws attention to those sounds and their spellings.

- If a student confuses the vowel sound, say something like, "What sound is most common for the letter *e*? Try it."
- If a student needs to try another sound, say something like, "Flip the vowel sound and try a different sound."
- If a student doesn't notice a long-vowel spelling, say something like, "Look across the word. What spelling do you notice? What sound should you try for the vowel?"

Progress Monitoring and Moving On

Start by focusing on target vowels for three to five sessions. When children achieve 80 to 90 percent accuracy during practice, move on. If children continue to struggle, assess their sound-spelling knowledge and phonemic awareness for any gaps.

Changing the Rigor	Type of Practice	Word Lists
START HERE	Which One?	To focus children's attention on the vowel, decrease the number of sound-spelling correspondences. Start with just three-sound words (for short *a*, use *pat* not *patch*, even if children know *-tch*).
INCREASE THE RIGOR	Word Building	Include all known sound-spellings.

5.4 How to Teach Decoding and Encoding Words With More Than Three Sounds

Purpose: To build children's decoding accuracy in words with more than three sounds by giving them targeted, repetitive practice in encoding.

Problem This Routine Solves

Sometimes, despite strong phonemic awareness and sound-spelling knowledge, decoding can still go haywire. After children can read CVC words, the complexity of words starts to increase rapidly: We introduce new sound-spellings (such as consonant digraphs) and add sounds to words (such as consonant blends). While some children continue making strides despite that, others need more instruction in how the English spelling system works.

Does this sound familiar?

Children might need additional practice moving beyond three sounds if they:

- Spell *task* as *t-a-s-ck* (making errors in new spellings) or *t-s-ck* (skipping the vowel).
- Decode *slug* as *sug* (skipping consonant blends).
- Decode *cats* as *cat* (skipping the final *-s*).

What the Research Says

Though there may not be a "magic bullet" in learning to decode, encoding practice is pretty close! When children encode, they segment a word into sounds and capture each sound with a letter. Research suggests that prioritizing encoding practice over decoding practice may lead to better orthographic learning, which is exactly what children who are skipping or confusing sounds need (Conrad et al., 2019; Møller et al., 2021; van Rijthoven et al., 2021). Indeed, encoding practice can improve every area of children's reading development, from phonemic awareness, decoding, and spelling to fluency, comprehension, and writing (Weiser & Mathes, 2011). Encoding practice is particularly helpful for children with and at risk of dyslexia (Hall et al., 2023). For this routine, children engage in word building. They build a word using letter tiles or magnetic letters and then change one sound or spelling to build a new word. This research-tested technique can improve phonemic awareness, encoding, and decoding (McCandliss et al., 2003).

Materials

- 5–10 letters (tiles or magnetics work best); one set per student
- Word list
- Elkonin boxes (as needed)

Routine (About 10 minutes)

Review. Give each student the 5 to 10 letters needed to build words. You do not need to give them the entire alphabet. Have them point to each letter and say its sound. If you are working with two- or three-sound spellings, have children construct these spellings (example: *ch*, *oi*, *ough*) and say the sound(s).

Teach. Reteach the challenging sound-spellings. For example, if children are consistently making errors with a new spelling, such as *ch* /ch/, say, "Remember, *c* and *h* together spell the sound /ch/."

If children are skipping a sound (for example, if they keep missing the second consonant in blends, no matter which spelling is involved), reteach segmenting: "We can hear each sound in a word by first saying the word, then saying it again slowly, and then saying each sound. It can help to count the sounds using your fingers or Elkonin boxes. Then we can represent each sound with a spelling." Model segmenting and then spelling two to three words.

Practice. Follow these steps for the word building. Aim for 10 to 20 words.

- Say the word. Children repeat the word.
- Children build the word by selecting letters for each sound.
- Check each child's word for accurate spelling. Prompt as needed.
- Say how to change the word. Give children explicit steps for each type of change (see below).
    - Change a spelling: Change the [letter name] to a [new letter name]. Read the new word to your partner.
    - Change a sound: Change the [sound] to a [new sound]. Read the new word to your partner.
    - Change to a new word: Change [word] to [new word]. Tell your partner what you changed.
- Children change the word by selecting new letters. Then children read the word to check and fix it if they are missing a spelling or sound.
- Check each child's word for accurate spelling. Prompt as needed.
- Repeat steps 4 to 6 for additional words.

Example

- Build *stuck*.
- Change *u* → *i*. Read the new word [*stick*].
- Change *stick* → *sick*. What did you do?
- Change the *s* → *l*. Read the new word [*lick*].
- Change *lick* → *click* by adding one letter. What letter did you add?
- Change *click* → *clip*.
- Change the *c* → *b*. What word is it now [*blip*]?
- Change *b* → *f*. Read the word [*flip*].
- Change *flip* → *flop*. What sound did you change?
- Change the last sound in *flop* → /k/. What word is it [*flock*]?

s t u c k
s t i c k
s i c k
l i c k
c l i c k
c l i p
b l i p
f l i p
f l o p
f l o c k

Steps to change words for word building:	To change a spelling (change the *t* to a *p*):	To change a sound (change the *a* to an *i*):	To change to a new word (change *mat* to *map*):
• Repeat the word. • Say each sound (use fingers to count sounds if necessary). • Select or write the letters that spell each sound.	• Point to the letter or spelling you're changing. • Select or write the new letter.	• Point to the sound. • Say the new sound. • Select or write the new sound.	• Say the new word while looking at your old word. • Point to the sound you're going to change. • Say the new sound. • Select or write the new sound.

Apply. Use sentence dictation. Say a sentence with one or two words from your word building list (other words should include previously learned sound-spellings and known high-frequency words). Have children repeat the sentence with you several times. Then have children write it. Be sure to briefly discuss the meaning of the sentence, especially with students learning English.

Prompt. Follow these guidelines:

- If a student is having a hard time getting started, say something like, "The word is ___. What word? What's the first sound? Write it."
- If a student skips a sound, say something like, "You were trying to spell the word *black*. You spelled the word /b/ /a/ /k/ *back* [point to letters]. What sound is missing? What letter spells that sound?"
- If a student uses the wrong spelling, say something like, "In this word, the /k/ sound is at the end, which often means it is spelled *-ck*. The /k/ sound in this word is spelled *-ck*."

Progress Monitoring and Moving On

With this routine, you may notice children's skill in a specific sound-spelling pattern improve in as little as a week. When they are encoding more than 90 percent of words correctly during word building, they have mastered the skill! Adjust your lessons to focus on application, such as decodable text reading and sentence dictation. Though this routine is designed to solve a common reading problem for some children, all children developing decoding skills can benefit from high-impact routines like this one.

Changing the Rigor	Phonemic Awareness Scaffolding	Directions During Word Building	Practice vs. Application
START HERE	Build words inside Elkonin boxes.	Say, "Change (word 1) to (word 2)" for each prompt.	Focus only on the practice section of this routine.
INCREASE THE RIGOR	Build words without boxes.	Move between prompts to change sounds, spellings, or words.	Include at least one sentence dictation.

5.5 How to Build Accuracy and Automaticity of Irregular High-Frequency Words

Purpose: To support children in reading and spelling irregular high-frequency words using explicit instruction and application.

Problem This Routine Solves

With explicit, systematic phonics instruction, many children thrive! Their skills and confidence skyrocket from decoding words such as *cat* to decoding words with more sounds and complex spelling patterns, such as *scratch*. And yet, somehow, the opposite seems to happen when it comes to irregular high-frequency words: Teacher after teacher has told me that children's high-frequency word reading suffers when they take a more serious phonics approach. Though it is not necessary to devote copious amounts of teaching time to high-frequency words, it may be beneficial to target them in small-group instruction, as needed.

Does this sound familiar?

Children might need additional practice with high-frequency words if they:

- Consistently confuse similar high-frequency words (read or spell *when* for *went*).
- Cannot remember irregular sound-spellings in particular words (read /w/ /a/ /s/ instead of /w/ /u/ /z/).

What the Research Says

High-frequency word knowledge is essential for children to become proficient readers and writers. About 300 high-frequency words account for 50 to 70 percent of all words children encounter in texts—children must be accurate and automatic when reading these words to be fluent readers (Green et al., 2024; Johns & Wilke, 2018; Mesmer, 2009). They fall into three categories based on sound-spelling correspondences. Many of them are regular, decodable words that children can learn through normal phonics lessons. Some are temporarily irregular, including a sound-spelling correspondence children will learn later in phonics. And finally, a few are permanently irregular, including a rare or unique sound-spelling correspondence.

High-Frequency Words		
A high-frequency word is a word that appears commonly in texts. They do not have to include irregular features or be a particular part of speech. Think about these words on a continuum:		
Regular high-frequency words include only regular sound-spelling correspondences that children know. *it* *can*	**Temporarily irregular high-frequency words** include at least one sound-spelling correspondence that children don't know yet. *is* (s as /z/) *down* (/ow/)	**Permanently irregular high-frequency words** include at least one sound-spelling that is rare or irregular. *of* *one*

(Miles et al., 2018)

Across all three categories of high-frequency words, the best way for children to learn these words is by matching sounds to spellings, for example, matching *w* to /w/, *a* to /u/, and *s* to /z/ in the word *was*. Explicitly teach children the irregular sound-spelling correspondences. Then help children use the regular and irregular sound-spelling correspondences to read and spell the word (Colenbrander et al., 2022; Dyson et al., 2017).

Materials

- Markers and whiteboards
- Word cards
- Text with target high-frequency word(s)

Routine (About 12 minutes)

Review. Using word cards, review previously taught high-frequency words. Prompt children to decode a word if they do not recall it.

Teach. To teach or reteach high-frequency words, start with your phonics program's scope and sequence for high-frequency words, or use the Children's Picture Book (CPB) Word List (Green et al., 2024), an updated high-frequency word list. Then use explicit language to describe the

Teach Irregular High-Frequency Words in Sets

If children continue to struggle with irregular high-frequency words, consider adjusting your scope and sequence to teach new or unusual sound-spellings in sets. Instead of teaching *me* and labeling the long *e* as irregular and then later teaching *he*, again labeling the long *e* as irregular, teach them together. Explicitly teach, "When a vowel is at the end of a two-sound word, it can spell the long sound." This will support stronger orthographic learning because it will help children read more than just one word.

Examples of high-frequency words that can be taught in a set	
Two-sound words with long final vowel sounds *me, he, she, be, no, go, so, we, see*	Words with the final *s* pronounced /z/ *was, as, his, has*

sound-spelling correspondences in the word(s): "We're learning two new words today: *me* and *he*. In these words, we can hear the first letter spell the sound we expect. The letter *m* spells /m/ in *me*; *h* spells /h/ in *he*. But the vowel spells its long sound: *e* spells /long e/."

Practice. Have children practice reading and spelling high-frequency words, prioritizing spelling for the most potential impact. Aim to have children practice decoding or encoding each word 10 to 12 times in a single session.

Practice Activities to Consider	
For accuracy:	**For automaticity:**
Map It! Say a word. Have students segment the word and draw a dot for each sound they hear. Then have them pick letters. Finally, have them spell the word.	***Quick Find*** Put 8–12 words in front of each student in a grid. Say a word and have students find it.

Based on Aspiranti et al., 2024

Apply. Have children read the high-frequency words in a controlled text. Check out Dr. Freddy Hiebert's TextProject, which has many texts designed to support high-frequency word knowledge. If you cannot find an appropriate text or wish to challenge children to spell more, engage children in one or two sentence dictations instead. Include multiple chances to spell the high-frequency words, but ensure the sentences are meaningful and grammatically correct. Other words in the sentence should be decodable or known high-frequency words.

Try This	Not This
He can see me.	He is excited to be with she and me.

Prompt. Focus on correcting spelling or pronunciation as necessary. With these irregular words, children may need to be reminded how sounds relate to spellings.

- For spelling: "Remember, in the word *there*, /air/ is spelled *ere*."
- For decoding, give mispronunciation support: "In the word *of*, *o* spells /u/ and *f* spells /v/: /uf/. *Of*. You try."

Progress Monitoring and Moving On

Though high-frequency word knowledge is essential, do not let yourself or your students go down a rabbit hole! Learning to read the word *are*, while important, means a student can read one word. Learning to decode means a student can read thousands of words. All of the routines in Chapters 5–7 build and support children's knowledge of irregular high-frequency words, as does their time spent reading. By definition, children will encounter high-frequency words every time they engage with a text. In other words, use this routine judiciously to target high-frequency word knowledge, along with other routines. When children can read high-frequency words in texts automatically, they no longer need additional explicit support.

Changing the Rigor	Practice	Application
START HERE	***Map It!*** (accuracy focus)	Decodable text with high-frequency words
INCREASE THE RIGOR	***Quick Find*** (automaticity focus)	Sentence dictation with target high-frequency words

In Closing, Remember This Swap...

Less "just use decodables" → More targeted support for decoding and encoding practice.

Learning to decode is hard work. It takes a lot of focus, practice, and support for children to succeed. Children must have many chances to decode words using their knowledge of sound-spelling relationships. One obvious way to give children lots of chances to decode words is with decodable texts.

In recent years, many educators have learned about the value of decodable texts and instituted a swap, such as this one in *Reading Above the Fray:* "More Decodable Texts, Fewer Non-Decodable Texts." This is a great and critical swap! But I've come to think of this as a "half swap"; it gets at what texts to use but does not fully describe how to support decoders. The texts we use do matter; however, instruction matters more. Instead of exclusively focusing on which text to use, focus on the specific instructional choices you make during a lesson. This includes giving additional explicit instruction on challenging sound-spelling correspondences, giving clear and immediate prompts, and adjusting the rigor of a lesson to better meet children's needs. These choices, outlined in the routines above, will ensure children practice exactly what they need to and receive the right amount of support to continue to grow in reading. If you aren't sure where to start, try focusing on how you prompt readers in decodable texts, using the prompts in Routines 5.1 and 5.2 for inspiration. Prompting might seem like a small move, but it is essential for helping your readers decode accurately.

Advancing Decoding Skills

CHAPTER 6

As children's word-recognition skills improve, they will begin recognizing and connecting larger units in words (Ehri, 2014), including vowel patterns, syllables, and morphemes, which is key for reading and spelling "big words." Readers who know and can flexibly use units in words are better at decoding and comprehending text (Bhattacharya & Erhi, 2004; Vadasy et al., 2006).

By third grade, 75 percent of the words children encounter in curriculum materials are multisyllabic (Kearns & Hiebert, 2022). To read a multisyllabic word, children need to know how to read single-syllable words. They also need to know:

- Vowel spellings that may represent multiple sounds (*e* can spell long *e* in *me* or short *e* in *pet*) and vice versa (long *e* can be spelled *e* in *me* or *ea* in *beat*).
- The spelling, pronunciation, and meaning of affixes, root and base words, and inflected endings.

A typical first-grade text and third-grade text containing multisyllabic words

Children also have to know how and when to apply those pieces of knowledge to read, spell, and understand multisyllabic words (Toste et al., 2017).

Furthermore, to advance decoding skills into multisyllabic words, we must increase our emphasis on word meaning. When children are just beginning to decode, they are for the most part working with words they've heard before (Tunmer & Chapman, 2012). As texts become more complex, however, they begin to encounter unfamiliar words. To orthographically map a word, or commit it to long-term memory, children need to connect the decoded form of that word to its meaning. Put simply, multisyllabic words are complicated!

What Do Children Need to Practice?

To advance decoding skills into multisyllabic words, children need to practice:

- Decoding two-syllable words by breaking up those words by syllable (Routine 6.1).
- Chunking words into decodable parts. To chunk words independently, they first need to practice it in small groups, with your feedback (Routine 6.2).
- Using morphemes to read, spell, and understand words. Children need to practice using morphemes (inflected endings, affixes, root/base words) to read, spell, and understand words (Routine 6.3).
- Adjusting vowel sounds in multisyllabic words flexibly. Vowel sounds are far less predictable in multisyllabic words than they are in single-syllable words (Kearns & Whaley, 2019). Children who have difficulty decoding multisyllabic words may need practice in adjusting their vowel pronunciation (Routine 6.4).

What About Spelling?

Want children to be better spellers? Teach morphemes—the smallest units of meaning in words! I often hear from third- through fifth-grade teachers that children's spelling is their top concern. Many of those children might be good readers. Many of them can spell words phonetically, but they can't spell them conventionally. If you want children's spelling to improve, lean into morphology instruction in whole-class and small-group instruction (Bowers & Bowers, 2018; Levesque et al., 2021). See Routine 6.2 and Heidi Anne Mesmer's *Big Words for Young Readers* for more information.

Furthermore, as children advance their word-recognition skills by decoding words in isolation, they need more practice decoding them in texts. They also need to be encouraged to make a connection to the word's meaning (Tortorelli et al., 2024). When it comes to teaching multisyllabic words, you should always keep that in mind.

More on Morphemes!

Routine 8.2 extends learning from Routine 6.2 by providing more practice with morphemes. Children move from decoding words to inferring their meanings. Check it out!

Logistics of Small-Group Instruction to Advance Decoding Skills

The most common questions I get about advancing decoding skills in small groups include:

- In which grade levels are children most likely to be advancing their decoding skills?
- Who needs small-group instruction in advanced decoding skills?
- How should I select texts?
- What should children do when they aren't in small groups?

In which grade levels are children most likely to be advancing their decoding skills?

Children in second through third grade are the most likely to benefit from instruction in this area, along with children in first grade if they have solidified single-syllable word recognition.

For children in fourth grade and above who need to solidify multisyllabic word recognition, be sure to include connections to word meaning. Research finds connecting word recognition and word meaning leads to more accurate and fluent reading (Austin et al., 2022). You may connect routines in this chapter to routines in Chapters 7 and 8 for a multicomponent approach to supporting older children's literacy.

Who needs small-group instruction in advanced decoding skills?

All children need explicit, systematic instruction in chunking multisyllabic words and in using morphemes to read, spell, and understand words. Even though many children in this category can read silently, they are more likely to learn the meaning and spelling of multisyllabic words if they pronounce them during text reading. Much like developing decoding skills, children benefit from practicing reading multisyllabic words in texts during small-group instruction and receiving feedback.

How should I select texts?

First, text selection matters! Children cannot become proficient readers by reading words only in isolation. When a text matches a child's background knowledge, that student is more likely to understand it and persist through challenging parts of it (Fulmer & Frijters, 2011; Smith et al., 2021). Plus, children who read (or listen to) books in content-area text sets are more likely to develop knowledge and vocabulary (Cervetti et al., 2016).

To select a text for advancing decoding skills, ask yourself these three questions:

- **Does it include multisyllabic words that children need to practice?** If you just taught the prefix *anti-*, make sure the text contains at least a few words with that prefix.
- **Can children read other words in the text with about 95 percent accuracy?** Try to select a text that is challenging, but not so challenging that children cannot engage with it. You do not need to use decodable texts or calculate decodability But you do need to determine if the text is accessible and appropriately challenging for the group you're considering.
- **Is the text's topic connected to content instruction or is it part of a topically connected text set?** If you are studying animal features in science, select a text on animal features. Alternatively, create a text set with at least six texts on a topic that interests the group to develop knowledge along with decoding skills (Cervetti et al., 2016).

To find texts that fit those criteria, consider the following sources.

- Passages from your ELA, science, or social studies curriculum
- ReadWorks
- Newsela
- Scholastic Knowledge Library
- *Scholastic News*
- Scholastic's *Storyworks*

Lean on AI for Texts

If finding texts is putting you in a pickle, try a generative AI platform such as Claude or ChatGPT to help you craft a text, using a prompt that spells out all your needs. Here's an example:

Write a well-crafted [grade level] text about [topic]. Make sure the text includes multiple examples of words with the morpheme [e.g., pre-, -ful, -tion*]. The text should include natural-sounding language. Include 6–8 target words with that morpheme.*

Don't forget to edit the text before you put it in front of children! Also, remember, there are legitimate ethical questions about using AI platforms that I cannot answer for you. Use at your discretion.

What should children do when they aren't in small groups?

Students learning to read multisyllabic words can practice many skills on their own or with a partner. Because multisyllabic word-recognition skills overlap with decoding skills and aspects of fluency, some students may still be reading certain words sound-by-sound, while others may be practically fluent but get stuck on three-syllable words. Consider what students can do and cannot yet do when selecting independent activities.

For students who are less skilled, use the activities from Chapter 5, Developing Decoding Skills. For example, have them play games with a partner or engage in partner reading.

For students who are more skilled, use activities from Chapter 7, Strengthening Fluency. For example, have them engage in partner fluency protocols or listen to ebooks.

Step-by-Step Routines for Advancing Decoding Skills

Advancing decoding skills to the point where students can read multisyllabic words effortlessly requires many things. It requires practicing those words in isolation and in context to strengthen students' connections between spellings, pronunciations, and meanings. It requires supporting students in being flexible. The routines in this chapter focus on strategies, practice opportunities, and applications that support and build multisyllabic decoding. They are not in a lockstep order; recall that not all students in this category will need significant support, so use small-group instruction strategically, especially for those students who do.

→ Go here to see a video demonstration of a Chapter 6 routine in action.

→ Go here for downloadable resources for these Chapter 6 routines.

6.1 How to Support Reading Two-Syllable Words Using Syllables

Purpose: To support children in decoding two-syllable words by providing targeted instruction in breaking up those words.

Problem This Routine Solves

We've all seen a student read words such as *land* and *fox* and then get completely flabbergasted by a word like *sandbox* a few minutes later. It often seems like children should be able to read and blend together these decodable parts, and yet, even basic two-syllable words can pose a challenge for some children. In one popular phonics program, decodable texts include compound words (like *sandbox*) by the end of kindergarten. Programs often say, "Teach children to break up a word," without much specificity about how children should break up the words or what to do when things go awry.

Does this sound familiar?

Children who struggle to read two-syllable words may:

- Decode single-syllable words like *sauce* but skip over or get stuck on words such as *napkin* or *robot*.
- Read only the first part of a compound word (*pan* for *pancake*).
- Use unhelpful parts to try to read longer words (notice *end* in *pretend* and try to decode *pret end*).

What the Research Says

Reading two-syllable words, including compound words, seems straightforward but includes new challenges for readers. Sometimes, children can accurately decode these words by blending individual sounds, but this can tax a child's working memory (Heggie & Wade-Woolley, 2017). Teaching children to break words into syllables can improve word recognition (Bhattacharya & Ehri, 2004; Moats, 2004). Using syllable types (e.g., open, closed, consonant-*le*) can help readers estimate the vowel sound.

Drilling children in syllable types or rules is not likely to be the most effective use of time (Austin et al., 2023). First, syllable types are estimates, not guarantees, about vowel sounds. Second, just looking at a word doesn't tell a student where a syllable break is: is it *rob / ot* or *ro / bot*? Instead of drilling students in syllable types or rules, explicitly teach them how words can be broken into syllables and which vowel sounds are most likely. Then give them steps to follow, such as the ones on the next page, to decode and encode words (O'Connor et al., 2015).

Steps to Take for Decoding and Encoding (Spelling) Words

Decoding	Encoding
1. Circle the vowels, vowel patterns, and/or vowel teams. Each vowel sound = one syllable.	**1.** Say the word slowly and count the vowel sounds you hear. Each vowel sound = one syllable.
2. Break up the surrounding consonants using the syllable guidelines.	**2.** Draw a line for each syllable.
3. Decode each syllable. Use the guidelines to estimate the vowel sounds.	**3.** Spell each syllable. Estimate the spelling of each vowel sound based on the syllable guidelines.
4. Put the syllables together and say the word.	**4.** Check to make sure you spelled each sound.
5. If needed: Return to Step 2 and break up the consonants differently to try new vowel sounds in Step 3.	**5.** If needed: Fix any spellings that do not match spelling conventions.

Syllable Types Explained

Syllable Type	Description	Examples
Compound words	Each word that forms the compound word usually follows its expected pronunciation.	*dog/house*
Closed syllables	A single vowel enclosed by consonants is usually short.	*cat* *roc/ket*
Open syllables	A syllable that ends with a single vowel is usually long.	*we* *o/pen*
Consonant-*le* final syllable	The final syllable in a word is consonant-*le*, and there is no other vowel.	*bat/tle*
Vowel patterns also seen in single-syllable words	Vowel patterns stick together and usually represent the expected vowel sound.	Silent *e*: *sur/pr**ise*** Vowel teams: ***oa**t/m**ea**l* *r*-controlled: *la/t**er*** Diphthongs: *str**aw**/berry*
Consonant patterns also seen in single-syllable words	Consonant patterns *often* stick together when dividing by syllables.	Digraphs: *ba**th**/tub* Beginning blends: *se/**cr**et* Ending blends: *la**nd**/fill*

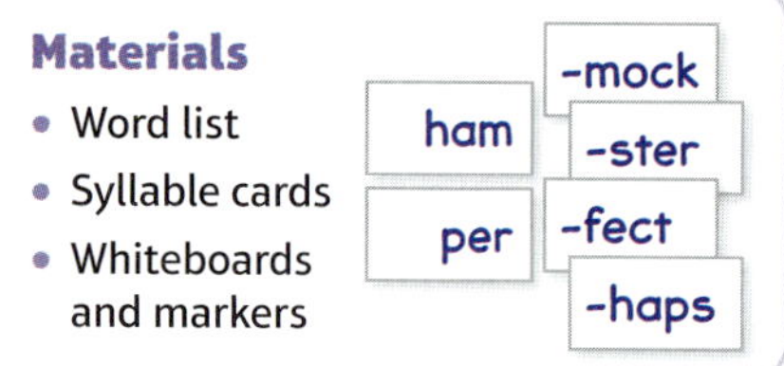

Materials

- Word list
- Syllable cards
- Whiteboards and markers

Routine (About 10 minutes)

Review (optional). Review previously learned syllable guidelines.

Teach. Teach and model using the syllable guidelines with steps. For example, show the word *silent* and say, "To decode this word, I will circle the vowels. There are two. Then I'm going to break up the consonants, making sure to keep spellings I recognize together. I think *s-i-l* and *e-n-t*. Now, let me read these two closed syllables: *sil ent*. That didn't work. Let me try *s-i* and *l-e-n-t*. Now, the first syllable is open because it ends with a vowel so it is probably the long sound. *Si lent. Silent.* Yes, that's a word I know. *Silent* means to be completely quiet."

Practice. Engage children in practice activities to decode and spell two-syllable words using the guidelines. Pick one of the practice activities below.

Practice Activities to Consider		
Make It, Read It	***Break It Up***	***Hear It, Spell It***
Show five cards with beginning syllables (*com, num, per, sun, re*). Show five cards with ending syllables (*mon, ber, son, set, do*). Have students put together each set to create the real words.	Show a two-syllable word (*water*). Follow the steps and have students break the consonants different ways (*wa/ter* and *wat/er*). Have students select the correct syllable breaks and pronunciation.	Say a two-syllable word. Have students repeat it and follow the steps to encode it on their whiteboard.

Inspired by Mesmer, 2024; Walpole & McKenna, 2017

Apply. Have children write a sentence of their choice that includes one or two words from the practice activity. Have each student share his or her sentence and discuss the meaning.

Prompt. Focus on supporting children in breaking words into syllables and using known sound-spelling correspondences.

- If a student splits a word into the wrong syllables, give a different syllable break: "*Mom ent* isn't a word. Let's try making the first syllable an open syllable and breaking after the *o*. Read the word now."
- If a student does not use conventional spellings, give information about the convention: "*Hammok* does have all the sounds you heard, but the final /k/ sound in the word is often spelled *ck* not *k*."

Progress Monitoring and Moving On

During your lessons, keep track of how many words children decode accurately and how often they self-correct if they use the wrong vowel sound. When you notice a student reading 90 percent or more of the words accurately, consider moving on to Routine 6.2.

Changing the Rigor	Practice Type	Syllable Guideline	Word Chunking Strategy Routine
START HERE	***Make It, Read It***	Compound words, closed syllables, and open syllables	Routine 6.1
INCREASE THE RIGOR	***Hear It, Spell It***	Consonant-*le*, vowel patterns	Routine 6.2

6.2 How to Support Chunking Multisyllabic Words in Texts

Purpose: To support children in chunking by providing explicit instruction in a flexible strategy to break apart words.

Problem This Routine Solves

To read multisyllabic words, children need chances to decode them in meaningful contexts and connect them to their oral vocabulary (Tortorelli et al., 2024). But when they encounter multisyllabic words, many children guess them or skip them, particularly ones with more than two syllables. And yes, they do need to read those words! By third grade, 19 percent of words in grade-level texts contain three or more syllables (Kearns & Hiebert, 2022).

Does this sound familiar?

Children who don't know how to break apart words may:

- Read "ha ... bit. Habit" for the word *habitat* (they may stop part of the way through the word and guess).
- Say a word that makes sense but is not the multisyllabic word on the page.
- Skip over multisyllabic words.

Children need a way to chunk, or break apart, multisyllabic words into smaller, decodable parts. Most curricula teach syllable rules to chunk words, which can be helpful, but this can lead to three problems:

- When it comes to words with three or more syllables, syllable rules can get wonky! One study found that some syllable rules lead to accurate decoding less than 50 percent of the time (Kearns & Whaley, 2019).
- Recalling and using syllable rules when reading very long words may take up so much cognitive effort that children's word recognition and comprehension could be negatively impacted (Kearns, 2020).
- Once children start learning affixes (often in second grade and beyond), syllable-based chunking alone may not lead children to use affixes they know. Instead, they need a flexible method that they can strategically deploy while reading to chunk any multisyllabic word.

What the Research Says

Researchers have studied at least eight teaching methods for chunking words (Kearns & Whaley, 2019), which boil down to these basic steps: break the word up, read the parts, try to pronounce the whole word, and fix it if need be. ESHALOV, or Every Syllable Has at Least One Vowel, is one method for chunking and decoding multisyllabic words. In one study, O'Connor and colleagues (2015) found that a protocol including ESHALOV led to increased fluency and decoding for middle schoolers with and without diagnosed reading disabilities. The steps for ESHALOV are below.

ESHALOV, Steps and Examples

Steps	Examples	Examples
1. Underline all of the vowels, joining any vowel patterns/teams.	predictive	chowder
2. Count the number of word parts to expect (number of vowel patterns/teams).	3 (*e*, *i*, *i-e*)	2 (*ow*, *er*)
3. If relevant: Identify any known parts, affixes, and roots/bases.	A child may say... Prefix: *pre-* Suffix: *-ive*	A child may say... Part: *chow* Part: *er*
4. Chunk the word into parts and decode each part.	*pre dict ive*	*chow der*
5. Try to pronounce the entire word.	*predictive*	*ch /long o/ der*
6. Flexibly try different vowel sounds if needed.	—	The child may need to correct the punctuation *ch /ow/ der*

Inspired by O'Connor et al., 2015

Routine (About 10 minutes)

Materials

- Reading passage with multisyllabic words
- List of 8–10 words from the passage

Review (optional). Review sound-spelling correspondences, morphemes, or syllable types you've taught. Show the spelling, morpheme, or part (for example, show an index card with the suffix *-ful*) and have children say the sound(s) and, for morphemes, the meaning.

Teach. Teach the ESHALOV strategy by saying, "This is one way that we can break apart a multisyllabic word we don't know. Then we can use our knowledge of decoding to figure out the word." Model the strategy with one to three words. Include the target vowel pattern and/or morphemes if needed.

Practice. Have children read the word list using the strategy. For the first few words, have them follow the steps with you. Then have them read the remaining words on the list independently or with a partner. If children do not know a word from the list, give a sentence containing the word or student-friendly definition of the word after the student decodes it.

Apply. Before children read the passage, quickly introduce it by making a clear connection to their background knowledge about the topic or text. Then have them read the passage using one of the recommended methods below. After reading, have children retell the passage.

Ways for Children to Read Together		
Choral Reading	**Partner Reading**	**Independent Reading With Support**
Best when students need constant support to apply the strategy.	Best when students are applying the strategy irregularly.	Best when students are successful with some multisyllabic words but still need support to use the strategy with some words.
Have students join you to chorally read the text. Pause at challenging multisyllabic words to lead them through ESHALOV.	Have students read in pairs. They may read chorally together or switch off after each sentence. Listen in and prompt when they get stuck. Also, remind them to offer help if their partner gets stuck.	Have students read to themselves, highlighting or circling challenging words as they go. Individually prompt when they get stuck.

Prompt. Focus on supporting children in using the steps of ESHALOV.

- If a student only reads part of a word, try: "Let's count the vowels. How many parts do we expect? Try each part again and blend."
- If a student skips the word or says a word other than what's on the page, try: "You can chunk this word into parts to make it decodable. Start by finding the vowels." Continue with all the steps of ESHALOV.

Progress Monitoring and Moving On

With strong core instruction in phonics and morphology, children can rapidly learn to use a new chunking strategy. Keep track of students' word-list reading during each lesson. When you notice a student becoming more automatic with multisyllabic words, move on to targeting morphemes (Routine 6.3) or fluency (Chapter 7).

Changing the Rigor	Text Reading Options	Text Selection	Number of Syllables in Practice Words
START HERE	Choral reading	Easy-to-understand, grade-level passage with limited number of multisyllabic words (10–20 percent of passage)	two or three
INCREASE THE RIGOR	Independent reading with support	Passage from your ELA, science, or social studies lesson	four or more

6.3 How to Support Chunking Multisyllabic Words With Affixes

Purpose: To support children in chunking by providing targeted practice using affixes to decode and spell words.

Problem This Routine Solves

Even when children know a lot about phonics, syllable rules, and chunking strategies, they may be missing a critical piece of multisyllabic word reading: morphemes, the smallest units of meaning within words. By third grade, about 60 percent of new words kids encounter have two or more morphemes (Kearns & Hiebert, 2022). Nonetheless, many children, particularly children with dyslexia, struggle to read, spell, and understand multimorphemic words.

Less advanced readers tend to rely on individual letters, while more advanced readers rely more on morphemes to read multisyllabic words (Archer et al., 2003; Shefelbine & Calhoun, 1991). A less advanced reader might try to read a word such as *reaction* letter-by-letter as *ree-k-t-ion*, while a more advanced reader knows to use the prefix *re-* and the base word *action*.

Does this sound familiar?

Children who don't know how to use morphemes may:

- Drop inflected endings (read *match* instead of *matched*).
- Decode morphemes incorrectly (read *unjust-ice* instead of *injustice*).
- Spell multimorphemic words incorrectly (spell *missunderstood* instead of *misunderstood*).
- Fail to connect morphemes to word meanings (read *immovable*, but say it means to move something again).

What the Research Says

Explicit instruction in the pronunciations, spellings, and meanings of morphemes improves children's reading, spelling, and comprehension (Austin et al., 2022; Colenbrander et al., 2024; Gellert et al., 2021). It is beneficial for typically developing readers, readers with dyslexia, and readers learning English. This routine can particularly benefit children learning English if you focus on cognates, such as the shared prefix *bi-* in *bicycle* and the Spanish *bicicleta* (Goodwin et al., 2013). All children benefit from practice putting morphemes together to create words, which builds skills in recognizing and spelling multimorphemic words (Toste et al., 2017; Toste et al., 2025). Because paying attention to morphemes requires paying attention to meaning, students should be given many opportunities to read and use multimorphemic words in sentences and texts.

Materials

- Word list
- Base word, affix, and inflected ending cards
- Maze sentences or connected sentences (one word in the sentence is replaced by two options that differ by one morpheme—for example, *preheat* could be replaced by *preheat/reheat*)

Routine (About 15 minutes)

Review. Review previously learned morphemes using root/base cards and affix cards. Have children read the morpheme and then say its meaning.

Teach. Explicitly teach the target affix or inflected ending by showing its card, pronouncing it, spelling it, and stating its meaning. Say, "This is the prefix *dis*-. *Dis*- is spelled *d-i-s*. It means not or opposite. Say *dis*-. Spell it. What does it mean?" Model chunking (breaking) the word into morphemes and telling the meaning of about three words with the morpheme. Tell the meaning of each part and say the whole word: "The base word *care* can mean attention and the suffix -*ful* means full of, so *careful* means full of attention."

Practice. Engage children in one of the practice activities below. Prompt them to focus on pronunciation, spelling, and meaning.

Practice Activities to Consider		
Blend a Word	***Word Matrix***	***Affix Web***
Hold up a base word card and have students read it. Define the word if needed. Show an affix or ending card and have students read it. Add parts together and have students say each part and blend together. Then have them define the word.	Give each student three affixes. Show a base word card and have the group read it. Define the base word if needed. Have each student add an affix to the base, read the new word, and define it. Tell the group if it is a real word or not. Build a word matrix around the base by moving all real prefixes to the left and all real endings/suffixes to the right.	Give each student three base cards. Show an affix word card and have the group read it. Define the affix if needed. Have each student add a base to the affix, read the new word, and define it. Tell the group if it is a real word or not. From there, build a web by writing the affix and real words on a whiteboard or using the cards.

Inspired by Ng et al., 2022; Toste et al., 2017; Walpole & McKenna, 2017

Apply. To solidify skills, children must apply knowledge of morphemes in context. They can do that by contrasting base words with similar morphemes through Maze sentence activities or by reading and writing connected sentences containing target morphemes. Prompt children to break words into morphemes using the ESHALOV strategy described in Routine 6.2. After each decoding attempt, ask them to define the word(s) with the target affix or ending.

Application Activities to Consider	
Maze Sentences Have students select the correct word to fit the context from two choices that differ by one morpheme: • Can you hand me that glass jar [*gentle* OR *gently*]? • I can't turn in my homework because it isn't finished. It is [*complete* OR *incomplete*].	***Connected Sentences*** Have students read connected sentences (two to three sentences about the same topic) with the target affix. Then have students write a sentence using a word with the target morpheme.

Inspired by Toste et al., 2017

Prompt. Focus on supporting children in using morphemes:

- If a student misses a known morpheme, try: "Do you see a part you know in this word?"
- If a student mispronounces a new morpheme again, try: "Remember, *r-e* is a prefix that we pronounce /r/ /long *e*/. Try the word again."

Progress Monitoring and Moving On

For children with persistent reading difficulties, affix instruction may not improve reading right away. Some effective programs include daily lessons for eight weeks of instructions, or 20 hours (Colenbrander et al., 2024; Filderman & Toste, 2022). Other children should progress more rapidly, especially if you coordinate small-group instruction with whole-class instruction.

Monitor progress with informal multisyllabic word lists. Toste and colleagues (2017) suggest the following goal for affix instruction: Children should read a list of 20 two- and three-syllable words with 95 percent accuracy and automaticity (reading each word in one second). When children meet that goal, provide them with more fluency-focused instruction.

Changing the Rigor	Morphemes	Application Type
START HERE	Inflected endings	Maze sentence task
INCREASE THE RIGOR	Common prefixes and suffixes	Writing sentences with target affix

6.4 How to Support Recognizing Vowels and Pronouncing Them

Purpose: To support children in attempting multiple vowel sounds during decoding by explicitly teaching a flexible vowel decoding strategy.

Problem This Routine Solves

The vowels in multisyllabic words can be a challenge. One letter could represent three (or more!) sounds (Kearns & Whaley, 2019). Take the word *marine*. Just by looking at it, a reader might think the *i* could reasonably represent:

- the long-*i* sound, as in *pine*
- the short-*i* sound, as in *sit*
- the schwa sound, as in the *i* in *pencil*

But no, it actually represents the long-*e* sound! Multisyllabic word recognition requires flexibility, particularly when it comes to vowel pronunciation (Bhattacharya & Ehri, 2004). Readers often must try more than one sound to arrive at the correct pronunciation. This is called vowel flexing.

Does this sound familiar?

Children who need more support with vowel flexing may:

- Read "cust /short *o*/ m ..." for *custom* (cannot flex to schwa sounds).
- Switch long and short vowels in syllables.
- Read *examine* as *ex am ine* and does not adjust from one spelling pronunciation to the real word (*missunderstood* instead of *misunderstood*).

What the Research Says

Even with adequate knowledge of phonics, syllables, and morphemes, readers can mispronounce a word. Accurate decoding leads to what researchers call the spelling pronunciation of a word. Spelling pronunciation is when a reader pronounces a word the way it is spelled, but not the way it is conventionally pronounced (Elbro et al., 2012). A common example of this is the word *Wednesday*, which is spelled *wed nes day* but pronounced *wenz day*. When reading complex words, readers may first try a spelling pronunciation, but then they need to adjust their pronunciation to match the real, spoken word (Heggie & Wade-Woolley, 2017).

Better word readers are more likely to link an inaccurate pronunciation to a real word. In other words, they recognize that something is "off." They try different vowel sounds, including the schwa, until they arrive at the word's true pronunciation. This kind of vowel flexing is an example of "set for variability," a skill strong readers possess, which I explain in Routine 5.3 (Steacy et al., 2019).

Materials

- Vowel chart
- Reading passage containing multisyllabic words with challenging vowels
- List of 8–10 words from the passage

Vowel Chart (example for spellings with the letter *a*)

Spelling	Sounds	Example Words
a	Short *a* Long *a* Schwa	cat acorn about
ai	Long *a* Short *a*	rain plaid
ay	Long *a*	play
au	/aw/ Short *a*	author laughter
aw	/aw/	awkward

Routine (About 10 minutes)

Review. Show recently learned or challenging vowel spellings. Have children say all possible sounds for the spelling.

Teach. Explicitly teach children that a target vowel spelling can represent multiple sounds. For example, "The spelling *ow* can spell /ow/ in *cow* or long *o* in *bow*."

Tell children to check vowel sounds after decoding (Edwards et al., 2025; Kearns & Whaley, 2019). Say, "After we decode a word and say it, we should think, 'Is this a real word or close to a real word?' We might need to try different vowel sounds to get to the right pronunciation of the word."

Practice. Have children read each word on the list, prompting them to adjust their vowel pronunciation as needed.

Apply. Introduce the text by making a clear connection to children's background knowledge about the topic or text. Then have them read the passage, prompting them to check the vowel and try a different sound if they get stuck on a multisyllabic word. From there, invite them to finish reading the text with a partner or independently.

Options for Supported Text Reading		
For children who need the most support: Select a text that is between 100–500 words. Have children whisper-read the entire text with your support during the small group.	**For children who need moderate support:** Select a passage that's long enough to start in small group and finish with a partner, usually about 250 words. Have children whisper-read the passage with your support during the small group. Then send children to finish reading the text with a partner.	**For children who need the least support:** Select several sentences from a larger text. Have children whisper-read the sentences with your support during the small group. Then send children to finish reading the text with a partner or independently.

Prompt. Focus on supporting children in flexibly trying multiple vowel sounds:

- If a student says the wrong sound for a vowel, try: Point to the vowel and say, "Try a different sound."
- If a student continues to say the wrong sound for a vowel, try: "Remember, *e* can spell three sounds: long *e*, short *e*, or schwa."

Progress Monitoring and Moving On

This routine is designed to be a quick, ultra-targeted experience. If children are having trouble adjusting pronunciations to real words, try carrying out this routine one to three times. Then continue to focus on vowel flexing in conjunction with Routines 6.1 and 6.2 to provide children with all they need to read multisyllabic words. Once they are reading multisyllabic words with about 90 percent accuracy, they may benefit more from fluency-oriented routines.

Changing the Rigor	Word List	Extending Beyond the Lesson
START HERE	Familiar, known words	Use this routine, along with Routines 6.1 and 6.2, to continue supporting multisyllabic words.
INCREASE THE RIGOR	Include some rare words, but be sure to define them.	Use this routine, along with the routines in Chapter 7, to strengthen fluency.

In Closing, Remember This Swap...

Less moving right into fluency → More targeted practice chunking and understanding multisyllabic words.

As children become more skilled in word recognition, we tend to take our foot off the pedal. Phonics programs often wrap up with syllable types and a few affixes by the end of second grade. Morphemes are often a footnote or a call-out box in upper elementary ELA curricula, but not a core component of instruction.

Instead, we tend to move from decoding straight into fluency or comprehension support. After all, it's easy to assume that children who know enough phonics will be great at reading "big" words. But even children who excel at decoding single-syllable words may have difficulty reading multisyllabic words (Toste et al., 2017).

If children are struggling to decode or spell multisyllabic words, the answer isn't more basic phonics or more fluency. The answer is to give more targeted practice chunking and understanding multisyllabic words. The routines in this chapter focus on different ways to support children practicing breaking up multisyllabic words to read them more accurately. If you aren't sure where to start, consider Routine 6.3. It is a great addition to whole-class morphology instruction to provide additional practice chunking words with morphemes, moving readers one step closer to proficiency.

Strengthening Fluency

CHAPTER 7

Fluency—reading with expression, automatic word recognition, rhythm, phrasing, and smoothness (Rasinski & Smith, 2025)—is one of the key goals of early reading instruction. It's also a powerful predictor of how well students will understand what they read (Kim et al., 2021; Torgesen & Hudson, 2006). When kids are fluent, their reading sounds natural—they move through words accurately and effortlessly, which frees them up to focus on meaning. That kind of ease comes from strong decoding skills (LaBerge & Samuels, 1974).

But fluency isn't just about speed or phonics—it also includes *prosody*, the intonation, stress, pacing, and rhythm that bring language to life (Benjamin & Schwanenflugel, 2010; Erekson, 2010). Prosody often gets overlooked, yet it's a vital part of fluent reading. And just as important, fluency depends on a basic level of language comprehension (Wolters et al., 2022). The bottom line? Children become fluent readers by reading—a lot.

What Do Children Need to Practice?

While independent reading and partner reading can improve fluency, adult-supported fluency instruction in small groups tends to be more effective (Burns et al., 2023; Downs & Mohr, 2025; Hudson et al., 2020; Maki & Hammerschmidt-Snidarich, 2022). Fluency practice in small groups can help all kinds of readers, from typically developing readers to readers with specific needs to English learners.

Supporting readers with clear, corrective prompts is essential to ensuring fluency gains transfer to new texts (Therrien, 2004). To improve fluency, children need to practice (and receive feedback):

- Reading at an appropriate pace (Routine 7.1).
- Reading with appropriate phrasing, smoothness, and attention to text features (Routine 7.2).
- Reading with expression (Routine 7.3).

Logistics of Small-Group Instruction to Strengthen Fluency

The most common questions I get about strengthening fluency in small groups include:

- How do I choose texts?
- How do I group children?
- How much time do I need?
- What should children do when they aren't in small groups?

How do I choose texts?

Choosing texts closely matched to students' abilities is critical to making fluency instruction impactful (Burns, 2024). First, think about matching texts to children's abilities in two parts: supporting accuracy and supporting knowledge.

Supporting Accuracy. Fluency instruction is most impactful when children can read the passage with 93 to 97 percent accuracy (Burns, 2024). Aim for passages that you're confident students will be able to read with ease. That said, know that it is okay if you don't select the perfect text. If the text seems a little advanced, pre-teach a few challenging words directly before reading to ensure sufficient accuracy and understanding (Burns et al., 2022).

Supporting Knowledge. When choosing texts, always keep the goal of fluency instruction in mind: to help students develop enough automaticity, accuracy, and expression for optimal comprehension. The goal of instruction is not "fluency for fluency's sake," but rather how improving fluency supports reading comprehension.

The routines in this chapter have one thing in common: They focus on repeatedly reading multiple texts across a topic. When students repeatedly read a single text, they are exposed to constrained vocabulary and syntax. But when they engage in wider reading, in which they read multiple texts across a topic, they have stronger vocabulary and comprehension growth (Kuhn, 2020). So plan a series of fluency lessons that have children read sets of, say, six passages on the same topic to support not only fluency but also comprehension (Cervetti et al., 2020). You can even select passages from your ELA, science, or social studies lessons to forge connections to content areas!

Second, think about selecting a passage or text that is matched to the task.

- For repeated reading: Select a passage that is between 100 to 300 words that children can read with over 90 percent accuracy. Repeated reading is best with short passages, partially because research indicates that repeated reading practice in small doses may best support growth (Ehlert et al., 2025).
- For Readers Theater: Select a script that is interesting to your students. If you are specifically targeting boys with low fluency and low motivation, try to find a humorous text (Young et al., 2021). Check the following resources for free scripts: Dr. Chase Young's website and the Iowa Reading Research Center. You can also create scripts from science, social studies, or ELA texts for an extra connection.

How do I group children?

Group students by their fluency goal based on assessment (see Chapter 2). The first goal of fluency instruction must be to increase speed if children are reading too slow. Use the prosody scale in Chapter 2 to determine appropriate goals. Fluency goals include:

- Reading at an appropriate speed.
- Reading in phrases.
- Reading with attention to text features, such as punctuation.
- Reading with appropriate expression.

Fluency instruction in small groups of up to six students is just as effective as one-on-one support for most readers. So aim for groups of six or fewer (Begeny et al., 2018).

How much time do I need?

Small-group fluency instruction should not take a significant amount of time. This chapter's routines are all about 15 minutes long. In reality, however, it isn't really "time in text" that matters. A student who reads 100 words per minute reads 500 words in five minutes. But a student who reads 25 words per minute reads 125 words in five minutes. The former student got four times as much practice as the latter. Indeed, it is the volume of text read that matters for fluency (Maki & Hammerschmidt-Snidarich, 2022; Therrien, 2004). Therefore, I suggest ensuring that slower readers receive more sessions a week—at least three.

What should children do when they aren't in small groups?

Students in this category, presumably, can read without intensive direct support from you. So independent reading beyond small-group instruction is the best support for fluency. However, bear in mind that when independent reading is unsupported (no clear purpose, no feedback, no partner support), it may not improve reading outcomes (Erbeli & Rice, 2022). So use partner reading protocols, such as SPORT, to help.

SPORT (Synchronous Paired Oral Reading Techniques). Pair a fluent reader with a less fluent reader and have them chorally read the text for a set period of time, up to 20 minutes. For a more in-depth discussion of SPORT, listen to Melissa & Lori Love Literacy Podcast, Episode #224, with Dr. Jake Downs.

Ebooks With Audio. One way to help students develop fluency is by allowing them to listen to texts. Doing that increases their exposure to text and provides a clear, fluent model (Kuhn & Stahl, 2003). But listening to someone else read isn't enough to strengthen fluency. Just like watching a basketball game doesn't make someone Stephen Curry, listening to books doesn't make children great readers. But it can give them a sense of "great technique." To improve fluency, children must also read!

Rereading. Immediately after the lesson, have students from one group (e.g., students with similar abilities) pair off and read the passage up to three additional times. If the passage is part of a longer text, have students continue reading the text with a partner.

Step-by-Step Routines for Strengthening Fluency

Supporting fluency means getting students reading more and giving clear feedback on their accuracy, speed, and expression. The routines in this chapter provide different ways to increase text reading with deliberate support for fluency. Start with Routine 7.1 to specifically support students in improving text reading pace. Then move into Routines 7.2 and 7.3 for more targeted support in prosody and to continue to build students' speed. For students with multiple needs in fluency, try mixing in multiple routines to keep them engaged. For example, spend Week 1 focused on Readers Theater (Routine 7.3) and then focus on pace (Routine 7.1) and phrasing (Routine 7.2) during repeated reading in Week 2.

➔ Go here to see a video demonstration of a Chapter 7 routine in action.

➔ Go here for downloadable resources for these Chapter 7 routines.

Two Key Types of Reading	
Choral Reading	Everyone reads together. Teacher and students read the text in unison.
Echo Reading	Teacher reads a section of text (sentence, stanza, or paragraph) and students read after, matching phrasing and intonation.

7.1 How to Improve Reading at an Appropriate Pace

Purpose: To increase children's reading rate with more targeted, repetitive practice.

Problem This Routine Solves

Although they may have strong decoding skills, some children read texts very slowly. Though conversations about fluency sometimes overemphasize speed, there is clear evidence that speed does matter. When children read with sufficient accuracy and speed, their comprehension improves (Schall et al., 2016). Some studies even find that speed is more predictive of reading success than other aspects of fluency (Bigozzi et al., 2017). When children read so slowly that it interferes with their comprehension, they need support in improving their speed.

Does this sound familiar?

Children who aren't reading quickly enough may:

- Read 10 WCPM slower than the 50th percentile.
- Be unable to retell a story despite accurate word recognition.
- Read slower than 35 WCPM in second or third grade; read slower than 90 WCPM in fourth grade or above.

We often think of reading speed while assessing words correct per minute (WCPM), which measures both accuracy *and* speed. For children who are not reading words accurately, see Chapters 5 and 6.

What the Research Says

About five decades of research support the use of repeated reading to improve fluency and comprehension. Some studies even show it outperforms multicomponent interventions and other types of evidenced-aligned interventions. In particular, repeated reading can improve reading speed (measured as words correct per minute) in many populations, including at-risk readers, readers with specific challenges, and multilingual learners (Stevens et al., 2017).

Repeated reading that is most likely to help readers includes careful text selection and lots of prompting. It also includes setting goals, such as "I will read five more words per minute by my last rereading today," which can increase not only fluency but also motivation and self-monitoring (Hammerschmidt-Snidarich et al., 2019; Morgan et al., 2012).

Routine (About 15 minutes)

Review (optional). Chorally read the passage from your last lesson with this group.

Teach. To begin, remind students their goal is to read at the pace of conversation by saying something like,"You can read like a grown-up by saying each word clearly and smoothly—just like you talk when you're having a conversation." Then model reading the passage fluently.

Materials

- Short reading passage (100–300 words)
- Goal setting and monitoring chart

Practice. Set a goal for this lesson. This goal should relate to reading rate and may be numeric (words correct per minute). Select a goal based on the group you're teaching: Numeric goals may be motivating for some children but may also overemphasize speed or be too stressful for others.

Goal Setting for Fluency

Rate over time (teacher-created numeric goal):	Rate for one session (student-created numeric goal):	Rate without numeric goal:	Rate for understanding:
Give each student a goal that aims to increase their WCPM score by 10–15 percent over the course of several lessons.	Have children set a realistic goal such as, "I will read 60 words correct per minute on my third reading of the passage."	Have children set a goal such as, • I will read like an adult. • I will read at a reasonable pace. • I will read the same way I talk.	Have children set a goal such as, • I will read fast enough to understand the passage. • I will reread if something doesn't make sense.

Set a goal with the group or with each child. Then chorally read the passage with the children, with proper intonation and speed. Read quickly, encouraging them to match your pace, intonation, and expression (Young et al., 2019). Then read the passage chorally again. When you've finished the second reading, ask a text-dependent comprehension question, such as, "What was this passage mostly about?"

Apply. In pairs or on their own, have children reread the passage two to three more times. Ask children to reflect on their goal and whether they met it. If time allows, have them retell the passage to their partner.

Prompt. Give direct feedback to children, encouraging them to read faster.

- If a student is still reading slowly: "Let's reread at a faster pace. Read the sentence along with me. Now, read it on your own."
- If a student is reading word by word: "Listen to me read this sentence smoothly, without breaks between each word. Now, read like me."
- If a student is making decoding errors: Use the Decoding Prompting Guide in the online resources. You might also consider if the passage is too challenging for fluency work and select an easier text for next time.

Extend the Lesson. After the lesson, have students work with a partner to read, reread, and retell a different passage on the same topic to further support fluency and encourage wide reading (Kuhn, 2020).

Progress Monitoring and Moving On

Most students you work with in small groups targeting speed and accuracy will need to make greater than average weekly growth. For example, a fourth grader beginning around 65 WCPM in the fall (between 25th–50th percentile) might aim to improve his fluency by more than one WCPM per week. If the student is not able to do that, consider increasing the amount of practice he receives with multiple repeated reading sessions per week or even per day. Remember, the best way to improve fluency is by giving the student more exposures to texts and reading them with your support.

Changing the Rigor	Text Genre	Text Selection	Practice vs. Application
START HERE	Short poems (under 300 words)	Select a passage that is easy to read (maybe even a decodable text).	Model and chorally read the text up to three times before allowing children to read it on their own.
INCREASE THE RIGOR	Passages from complex texts, including informational texts	Select a passage from a complex text, up to one grade level above skill.	Model and chorally read the text once before allowing children to read it on their own.

7.2 How to Improve Phrasing When Reading Text Aloud

Purpose: To help children improve phrasing by providing targeted practice reading in phrases.

Problem This Routine Solves

Fluent readers read like we speak, but many children struggle to do that. They may read one word at a time, pause at odd moments while reading a phrase or sentence, or not pause at all between words, phrases, or sentences. Reading that way may interfere with optimal comprehension (Kim et al., 2021). If children score 1 or 2 on the Multidimensional Fluency Scale in Rhythm and Phrasing and/or in Smoothness, they may benefit from support in phrasing.

Does this sound familiar?

Children who need support in phrasing may:

- Read word by word, haltingly or robotically
- Pause for a long time at random moments.
- Read without any pauses between words, phrases, or sentences.

Reading prosody, which includes phrasing, rhythm, and expression, tends to develop after children can read accurately and automatically, usually in second grade (Miller & Schwanenflugel, 2008). To be efficient and effective, target prosody after children have solidified decoding skills and are reading at a reasonable rate.

What the Research Says

Much of the research that applies to the last routine applies to this one—most importantly, reading can improve reading fluency! Pairing repeated reading with explicit instruction that targets prosody works best (Shhub et al., 2023). To significantly improve children's prosody in general and phrasing in particular, try phrase-cued reading, or reading a text with phrases marked (Levasseur et al., 2006; Rasinski, 1990; Rodgers et al., 2025). Theoretically, phrase-cued reading, as described in the following routine, helps children understand the syntactic and semantic elements necessary to read with appropriate phrasing.

Materials

- Reading passage with phrases marked with slashes or swoops

slashes

But Eric was not ordinary. /He was extraordinary. /In fact, /he could do magic.

swoops

1
Do not walk in that huge hole!

2
Do not walk in that huge hole!

Routine (About 10 minutes)

Review (optional). Chorally read the passage from your last lesson with this group.

Teach. Explain why we read in phrases: "We're going to practice reading phrases rather than word by word. This helps reading sound more natural so it is easier to make sense of the words on the page." Then show how to use the phrase markings: "I've marked phrases in our passage that we can scoop up all together." Model reading the passage fluently, pausing at the slashes or the end of each swoop.

Practice. Have children practice reading a few phrases from the passage rather than the entire passage. Say, "We can scoop up an entire phrase instead of reading one word at a time. Let's try." Select two to three phrases for children to read chorally with you two times. Then have children echo-read the passage.

Apply. In pairs or on their own, have children reread the passage two to three times, focusing on scooping phrases and pausing between phrases. If time allows, have children retell the passage to their partner. Ask a basic, text-dependent comprehension question, such as, "What was the problem in this story?"

Prompt. Give precise feedback to encourage proper phrasing.

- If a student is reading word by word: "Let's reread that phrase. Listen to me scoop the whole phrase. Now you try."
- If a student is pausing too long between phrases: "Take a quick breath and scoop your next phrase."
- If a student is making decoding errors: Use the Decoding Prompting Guide. You might also consider whether the passage is too challenging for fluency work and select an easier text for next time.

➔ Go here to download the Decoding Prompting Guide.

Progress Monitoring and Moving On

Look for movement on the Multidimensional Fluency Scale on page 34, particularly for rhythm and phrasing, and/or for smoothness. Or, after each lesson, ask yourself: Does this reader attend to phrasing? Once you mark "Yes" for a student three to five times in a row, she may be ready to move on.

If students are not demonstrating any improvements within a few weeks, consider increasing the amount of practice, particularly with a peer, using continuous texts. It may also be beneficial to provide more explicit instruction and practice in syntax. (See Routine 8.2.)

Changing the Rigor	Support
START HERE	Provide a clear model and echo-read the entire text up to three times.
INCREASE THE RIGOR	Model and echo-read part of the text (for example, one stanza of a poem) before releasing children to read and reread with a partner.

Using the Structure of This Routine for Other Instructional Targets

This routine can be used to target any aspect of fluency by adjusting the teaching point and type of practice.

Target	Teach	Practice
Reading smoothly	"We can read just like an adult by confidently pronouncing each word, like we're having a conversation, and matching our voice to the meaning in the passage."	Choral or echo reading of the entire passage.
Reading known words automatically	"When we get up to a word we already know, we can just read it right away. We don't need to decode it! Sometimes, it helps to take a big breath before a sentence or to reread a sentence to feel confident."	Choral reading of a word list (of words from the text) with automaticity.
Reading with respect for punctuation	**Basic:** "When we're reading, it's important to notice punctuation. Whenever we get to punctuation, we can take a breath." **Intermediate:** "When we notice a question mark at the end of the sentence, we can raise our voice as if we were asking a question. If you notice a question mark after you've read a whole sentence, you can go back and reread it to add in the change in your voice." **Advanced:** "This is an ellipsis. Ellipses are used by authors to signal a pause or show that something is incomplete or in progress. They sometimes tell us that we should be anticipating something or wondering about something. When we see an ellipsis, we can let our voice trail off. If we're reading something scary, we can also say 'duh duh dun!' in place of the ellipsis to show fear."	Choral or echo reading of sentences with target punctuation.
Reading to emphasize meaning	"When we read a story, we match the emotion in the story to our voice." "When we read informational texts, we may primarily use a confident, calm voice without a lot of emotion."	Choral or echo reading of the entire passage.

7.3 How to Improve Expression When Reading Text Aloud

Purpose: To help children improve expression with high-interest Readers Theater.

Problem This Routine Solves

For some students, it may be awkward, embarrassing, or dull to read short passages with expression. After all, most of the time, proficient readers read silently. Yet, research does find a correlation between oral reading prosody and silent reading comprehension, confirming that even as children gain proficiency in silent reading, it is important to continue supporting oral reading prosody (Rasinski et al., 2011). For repeated reading that may feel more authentic and motivating for your readers, this routine features practicing and performing scripts (also known as Readers Theater).

What the Research Says

In Readers Theater, children read a script over the course of several sessions and then perform the script for a real audience—and, in the process, improve their fluency, word recognition, and comprehension (Garrett & O'Connor, 2010; Young et al., 2019). Furthermore, Readers Theater can improve children's motivation and confidence in reading (Clark et al., 2009). Though most Readers Theater scripts are narratives, consider incorporating nonfiction scripts to build children's knowledge of various topics (Garrett & O'Connor, 2010; Young & Rasinski, 2009; Uribe, 2019). Readers Theater can support children with various strengths and needs, including children learning English, children with reading difficulties, and struggling readers in middle and high school (Keehn et al., 2008; Mastrothanasis et al., 2023; Uribe, 2019). Young and his colleagues (2021), for example, found that fluency practice focused on Readers Theater led to substantial growth in decoding, vocabulary, and comprehension for boys, most likely because of features such as collaboration and dramatic performance.

Routine (10–15 minutes)

Readers Theater is a multi-day experience: about 10–15 minutes over four to five days. If you are short on time, reduce practice to two days. You may also allow children to practice on Day 4 without your direct support, if they were successful on Day 3.

Materials

- Readers Theater script for reading
- A real audience (at a minimum, have students perform for classmates)

Day 1: Teach. Select one or two prosodic elements to focus on, such as punctuation and smoothness, and teach each of them explicitly (see the chart in 7.2 for options). Say: "When we come to an ellipsis, it's a signal for us to pause. If we're reading fiction, it might mean that the character is thinking, scared, or excited. After the pause, we may need to change our voice to match the meaning. Say: if we're reading a story in which the character is nervous, we might pause at an ellipsis and then begin reading in a shaky voice." Model reading the entire script. Pause as you read to "think aloud" about your target prosodic elements. Model reading once more with full expression.

Days 2–4: Practice. On Day 2, have children practice chorally reading the text. Then, as a group, summarize the text. Ask children to circle any unknown words and define them using a child-friendly explanation, giving an example or non-example of each word, and providing a sentence containing the word. Then have children select their roles for Day 5's Readers Theater performance.

On Days 3 and 4, have children read their parts orally at least three times, focusing on reading expressively, accurately, and at an appropriate pace. Give feedback as children read and have them echo-read sections that are challenging.

Day 5: Apply. Performance time! Have children perform the script for an authentic audience: classmates, students from another class, other teachers, administrators, or visitors. To extend the performance, children can define unknown words (from Day 2), summarize the script, or share their favorite part of the experience.

Prompt. Give direct feedback to children to encourage expression while reading.

- If a student is pausing at awkward moments: "Remember, we're working on reading smoothly. Listen to me read this sentence smoothly, without breaks. Now, read like me."
- If a student is skipping punctuation: "What punctuation mark do you see in this sentence? [a comma] What should we do when we see a comma? Reread the passage and show me what to do when you come to a comma."
- If a student is not capturing the right emotion: "How does your character feel at this point in the script? How can you match your voice to the emotion?"

Progress Monitoring and Moving On

If you're working with students who need to improve their reading expression, plan to use at least six different Readers Theater scripts over a period of six weeks or more. Research shows that this kind of sustained, repeated practice is necessary before you'll see noticeable growth in expressive reading (Keehn et al., 2008; Young et al., 2019). Use the Multidimensional Fluency Scale on page 34 (particularly the Expression section), along with WCPM, to monitor improvements in students' fluency. If children perform at grade level, move them from small-group instruction to whole-class fluency support and monitor for additional needs.

Changing the Rigor	Text Types	Text Length	Support
START HERE	Narrative Readers Theater scripts	Script can be read in less than five minutes.	Provide feedback and support through all five days.
INCREASE THE RIGOR	Readers Theater scripts created from classroom science or social studies materials	Script can be read in five to 10 minutes.	Reduce practice time from three to two days. Release group to practice without your direct support.

In Closing, Remember This Swap…

Less rereading at random for fluency → More targeted repeated reading practice

Fluent reading is a major goal of early reading instruction. When children read a text fluently, they read words accurately and effortlessly and their reading sounds smooth and expressive. Fluency relies on the coordination and automaticity of many skills and knowledge. So targeting fluency in small-group instruction means providing children specific instruction and support for different aspects of fluency. Crucially, it also means providing children more time in texts.

There is a subtle but critical difference between gathering children in a small group to re-read a text three to five times and gathering children in a small group, setting a clear goal around reading rate, and engaging in choral, repeated reading with precise prompts. Rereading a text without a clear purpose and support may not be the best use of time or the best support for fluency. Instead, focus on precision. In all of the routines in this chapter, you'll notice a focus on precise, explicit instruction or goal setting around an aspect of fluency, careful text selection, different types of practice, and immediate, precise prompting. If you aren't sure where to start, begin with children who need to improve their reading rate. Use Routine 7.1 to ensure repeated reading is as targeted as possible, strengthening children's fluency and, over time, their comprehension.

CHAPTER 8

Deepening Language Comprehension With Complex Texts

Language comprehension is a complex web of knowledge, skills, and strategies that develop over time. It must be supported early and often throughout elementary school. Children do not learn to read (develop word recognition) and then read to learn (develop language comprehension): They are developing language comprehension all along (Duke et al., 2021)! That said, it's important to keep in mind that as their word recognition, as well as fluency, improves, children are expected to read more complex texts, which often pose new demands on their comprehension. Those texts include words, sentences, and structures that may be difficult for children to understand and navigate (Duke et al., 2021). Furthermore, in most complex texts, some information is not explicitly stated and, therefore, must be inferred, which can also be difficult (Rice & Wijekumar, 2024). The goal of this chapter and its routines is to help you support children so they can comprehend complex, grade-level texts.

What Do Children Need to Practice?

First, children need many opportunities to read complex texts and to build knowledge (Peng et al., 2024). Second, they need skills and strategies to navigate characteristics of those texts (Duke et al., 2021). For that to happen, we must first determine what makes a particular text difficult for a student. Then we can provide targeted instruction and support in skills and strategies. In the chart below, I list characteristics that may be difficult for readers and practice opportunities to make things easier. This list is not exhaustive; it focuses on a few key areas that are often under-taught, yet support meaning making and can improve with practice and feedback.

Characteristic of Text	Why It Might Be Difficult for a Reader	What Readers Can Practice
Vocabulary	A reader may not know the meaning of key words.	Inferring the meaning of unknown words through morphological analysis and/or context.
Syntax	A reader may have difficulty understanding sentences with features such as clauses, modifiers, and phrases.	Building sentences and taking them apart to understand how ideas connect.
Text Organization	A reader may have difficulty navigating the structure of a text and understanding why the writer chose its structure (e.g., to tell a story, to make an argument).	Identifying and using structure to give a retelling, generate inferences, and summarize the text.

Logistics of Small-Group Instruction to Deepen Language Comprehension With Complex Texts

The most common questions I get about deepening language comprehension in small groups include:

- How does small-group instruction relate to whole-class instruction?
- How do I choose texts?
- Who will benefit from these routines?
- What should children do when they aren't in small groups?

How does small-group instruction relate to whole-class instruction?

Just as small-group instruction in word recognition relates to whole-class phonics instruction, small-group instruction in language comprehension relates to read-aloud, ELA, science, and social studies whole-class instruction. When small-group instruction aligns with whole-class reading instruction by focusing on the same content and teaching the same processes and strategies for engaging with texts, struggling readers can build more knowledge and vocabulary (Stevens et al., 2020). To align instruction, use topically connected texts (see next question) and, in both contexts, teach the same processes and strategies for navigating difficult passages.

How do I choose texts?

One of the goals of small-group instruction is to enable students to access texts used in and content covered in whole-class instruction. The key to making that happen is text selection! Consider these options.

Use challenging passages from whole-class instruction in small-group instruction. This is a particularly powerful practice! First, identify what makes the passage difficult for a group of students. Then, with that group, pre-teach elements from the passage to enable students to access it.

Select passages that are topically aligned with content-area instruction. If children encounter difficulties, give them additional supported practice, along with knowledge-building opportunities. Selecting texts on the same topic that are slightly easier for children to access can help (Strong et al., 2018).

As a starting point, it's okay to use Lexile or other metrics that estimate text complexity. But be aware of what those metrics can and cannot tell you. Lexile, for example, assigns an overall score based on sentence length and word frequency (Graesser et al., 2014), but you need to consider other aspects of the text—and that starts with knowing what you want your students to practice:

If you want them to infer the meaning of words, select content-connected passages so children interact with vocabulary they can use in ELA, science, and social studies (Cervetti et al., 2023; Hwang et al., 2023; Nielsen et al., 2022).

If you want them to use text structure to understand texts, select passages that clearly represent a particular text structure, such as compare and contrast, or problem and solution. Then move into passages with less transparent structures. To determine the clarity of a text's structure, ask yourself questions such as, "Is the organization straightforward and consistent? Is the author's purpose for writing the text obvious?" (Fisher & Frey, 2014).

Who will benefit from these routines?

Remember, language comprehension is not a phase after word recognition. Children benefit from instruction in comprehension at every age and stage, but the routines in this chapter are likely most useful after decoding is solidified and children are experiencing challenges with more complex texts.

Keep in mind that not all children will need small-group instruction focused on language comprehension. In fact, you're likely to be effectively teaching many of the skills involved—such as understanding vocabulary, interpreting complex sentence structures, generating inferences, and using text features to make meaning—during whole-group instruction. The routines in this chapter are designed to help provide additional, targeted practice for children who are not able to adequately understand grade-level texts during your whole-class comprehension instruction.

What should children do when they aren't in small groups?

Students who are deepening language comprehension to improve access to complex texts should be engaged in reading continuous text even when they are not in a small group.

But independent reading needs structure. Simply saying, "Go read!" isn't enough. Students benefit most when independent reading time includes clear purpose, choice, and accountability. In fact, one study found that sustained silent reading alone—from kindergarten through twelfth grade—did not lead to measurable gains in reading achievement (Erbeli & Rice, 2022).

Partner Reading. Pair a more fluent reader with a less fluent reader. Have the more fluent reader read the passage first, and then have the less fluent reader repeat the reading. Finally, have both readers retell the story to one another or share key details from an informational text (McMaster et al., 2006; Musti-Rao et al., 2009).

Reading to Extend Knowledge. Give students a set of topically related texts to pick from and a clear purpose for building knowledge. It might sound like this: "While you're working on your own, read about key people in the American Revolution. After you read, choose one person and complete this graphic organizer about that person. Bring your graphic organizer to social studies to get a jump start on our biography project."

Writing About Reading. Writing is one of the best independent activities to improve students' reading (Graham & Harris, 2018; Tortorelli & Truckenmiller, 2024). When students write about what they've read, even if it's just a summary, their comprehension improves. So at the end of your small-group lesson, when you send students off to work independently, give them a writing prompt based on the text they read with you (Graham & Hebert, 2010).

Step-by-Step Routines for Deepening Language Comprehension With Complex Texts

For these routines, I focus on common language comprehension challenges that students encounter when they read complex texts. I start at the word level, offering strategies for inferring the meaning of unknown vocabulary. Then I move to the sentence, suggesting ways to help students make sense of how words fit together syntactically. Lastly, I move into comprehending a whole text, offering research-proven strategies to understand text organization and generate inferences to unlock deeper comprehension. Keep in mind, the routines must always be in service of developing knowledge or deepening text comprehension, and not of mastering strategies for the sake of mastering strategies.

8.1 How to Strengthen Understanding of Unknown Words

Purpose: To support children in inferring the meaning of new words in texts.

Problem This Routine Solves

Children need to learn about 2,000 to 3,000 new words every year to become proficient readers (Anderson & Nagy, 1993; Brysbaert et al., 2016). But vocabulary-focused ELA programs show us how to teach only about 400 words a year. While direct instruction has its place, most new words are likely learned through rich language experiences, including text reading (Brysbaert et al., 2016). Said another way, children must be able to learn new words from the texts they are reading.

Does this sound familiar?

Children who may benefit from practice inferring word meanings may read a sentence such as, "They decided to leave because the noise was unbearable," and think:

- *Unbearable* means "not about bears."
- *Unbearable* means "kinda loud."

Even if they can successfully decode a word, children might not be able to tell its meaning when they encounter it in a text. Why is that a problem? In the upper grades, the most important words in a text—the words that children need to comprehend the text and build knowledge—are often words they can decode but don't understand, or words they skip entirely (Toste et al., 2017).

What the Research Says

In addition to explicit vocabulary instruction, children need to figure out the meaning of unknown words to learn vocabulary successfully (Cervetti et al., 2023). Moreover, children are more likely to use those strategies when reading on their own.

There are two primary sources of information that can help a reader figure out a new word's meaning: morphological information and contextual information (Nagy & Scott, 2000; Nielsen et al., 2025).

Morphological Information: When children can identify morphemes in words, and can use them to determine a word's meaning, they become better at learning new words and at comprehending the text (Levesque et al., 2019).

Contextual Information: When children can infer word meaning using context, they become better at storing vocabulary in long-term memory and comprehending the text (Nash & Snowling, 2006).

Studies show that a combined morphological/contextual approach has the potential for improving word learning. When children are better at learning words, they may also better understand complex texts.

Hang On, Isn't This the Same as Three-Cueing?

Nope! The focus of this routine is not on decoding but on understanding meaning. When children encounter an unfamiliar word, we want to guide them to first decode and then infer the meaning at the word level (using morphemes) and at the sentence level (using context) (Perfetti & Stafura, 2014).

Materials

- Base word, affix, and inflected ending cards
- Maze sentences
- Reading passage

Routine (About 15 minutes)

Review. Review previously learned morphemes with root/base and affix cards. Have children read the morpheme and then say its meaning.

Teach. Explicitly teach children to use morphemes and context to understand unknown words (adapted from Nielsen et al., 2022):

1. Show a sentence with an unfamiliar word. Read it to students, pausing at the word. Then have students read the sentence silently and whisper-read the unfamiliar word.
2. Encourage them to look for helpful information from morphemes: "Chunk the word into morphemes and tell the meaning of each part. Tell what you think the meaning of the word is."
3. Next, encourage students to look for helpful information in the context: "Scan the text or sentence right before and after the unfamiliar word. Tell what you think the context tells you about the meaning of the word and if the meaning is different from what you thought in Step 2."
4. Tell them to combine both pieces of information: "What do you think the meaning of the word is?"

Practice. Have children practice the word-learning strategy with Maze sentences (Nielsen et al., 2022; Toste et al., 2017). Ask them to select the correct word to fit the context from two choices that differ by one morpheme by analyzing the morphemes and looking for helpful information in the context.

Example

- Read the sentence with *unfamiliar*. Then reread with *familiar*.
- Chunk the words *unfamiliar* and *familiar*. Tell the meaning of the parts. Tell the meaning of each word.
- Scan the text that comes before and after the words for helpful information. Tell what the context indicates about the correct meaning of the word.
- Select which word (and morpheme) matches the correct meaning of the word.

The man was **unfamiliar/ familiar**. Olivia had never met him before.

Apply. Select a passage from an ELA, science, or social studies text that contains an unknown word or words. Introduce the passage's topic by making a clear connection to prior knowledge or by quickly explaining a core concept. Then have children read the passage, prompting them to use the word-learning strategy to understand an unfamiliar word. After supporting children in making sense of a few words, send them to finish reading the text with a partner or independently.

Prompt. Support students as they use the word-learning strategy.

- If a student cannot break the word into morphemes, help them find morphemes and define them: "Remember, we can look for parts that we know. In the word *unfamiliar*, we know the part *un*. What does that prefix mean?"
- If a student struggles to identify useful context information, point out helpful information such as key words: "In the next sentence, I see *never*. Since the prefix *un*- means *not*, I'm thinking the right word might be *unfamiliar*."

Progress Monitoring and Moving On

Like other elements of reading that connect to comprehension, children might not "move on" from applying this strategy; instead, think about how you might use this routine to help bolster children's awareness and understanding of unfamiliar words. You might teach this strategy over several lessons and then remind children to apply it when they read throughout the year.

Changing the Rigor	Morphemes	Context
START HERE	Words with two morphemes	Sentences with clear context information about word meanings
INCREASE THE RIGOR	Words with three or more morphemes	Sentences with vague context information

8.2 How to Strengthen Navigating Complex Syntax

Purpose: To support children in understanding complex syntax by combining and deconstructing sentences.

Problem This Routine Solves

Consider these sentences: "Timothy went to get his brother's coat. He was cold." Who was cold? Was it Timothy? Or his brother? Or a third party? A reader's ability to infer who "he" refers to is an anaphoric inference (when the author replaces one word in a text with a different word—in this case, a referential pronoun). Or this one: "After the movie ended, we went out for ice cream." The adverbial clause in this sentence (after the movie ended) comes before the main clause (we went out for ice cream). Children might get confused about the order of events or fail to understand the relationship between clauses, particularly if they are not paying attention to the connective, "after" (Zipoli, 2017). Connectives are cohesive devices (including conjunctions and adverbs) that link ideas and information within and between sentences (Crosson & Lesaux, 2013). Even when children can fluently read a sentence and define each word, they may still have difficulty understanding the relationship between ideas.

Does this sound familiar?

Children who have difficulty navigating complex syntax to put ideas together may respond to directions such as these.

Direction	Child's action or thought
Before you turn in your paper, get out your red folder. (connective)	Student turns in paper and then gets out folder.
Ms. West needs to go see the school secretaries. She is needed by them. (referential pronouns)	Student doesn't know who Ms. West needs.

What the Research Says

Syntax, a key element of language comprehension, is the system for organizing words into meaningful phrases, clauses, and sentences, according to the rules of that language. Sentences with elements such as dependent clauses, prepositional phrases, and referential pronouns can be hard to understand. In fact, so much meaning is held in these sentence parts that understanding at the sentence level is just as important to reading comprehension as vocabulary is (Deacon & Kieffer, 2018; MacKay et al., 2021; Nielsen et al., 2025). Understanding each sentence, and how it relates to the next sentence, is essential to understanding texts!

Despite recognizing the importance of the sentence, researchers aren't all that clear about how to improve children's understanding of syntax. We do have evidence that interventions that combine explicit instruction in syntax along with other aspects of comprehension benefit readers, including English learners (Proctor et al., 2020; Silverman et al., 2020; Zipoli, 2017). Promising practices include explicit instruction in challenging sentence structures and elements, such as in understanding connectives and referential pronouns. In particular, practice in building sentences (e.g., combining simple sentences into more complex sentences) and taking them apart (e.g., breaking complex sentences into simpler sentences) can improve sentence writing and may support sentence comprehension (Graham & Perin, 2007; Saddler, 2012; Saddler et al., 2018).

Routine (About 15 minutes)

Materials

- Short reading passage related to content-area learning
- 3–5 pairs of sentences from the passage to build and take apart
- Highlighters, pens, or pencils

Review. Introduce the passage by reviewing key content (vocabulary, other background knowledge) critical to understanding this text.

Teach. Tell children that, to understand this text, they will need to read some complex sentences. Teach children to notice complex syntax and referential pronouns. Start by explaining what a pronoun is: "A pronoun stands in for a noun so we don't have to name the noun over and over again." Then model the metacognitive steps students should take by thinking aloud: "Wait, I just read 'Before the party, he went to the grocery store.' I need to stop and make sure I know who he is. He is our main character, Ahmad. I also noticed the author gave me extra information. Ahmad didn't just go to the store, he went to the store first and then to the party."

Practice. Model how to build sentences and take them apart and then support children as they try it on their own (Zipoli, 2017). Follow up with questions about the relationship between ideas in the sentences and clauses, such as, "Whose dog is snuggling?" or "Who was angry? Why?"

Sentence Combining	Sentence Deconstructing
Have children combine sentences, which can include adding or eliminating connectives and referential pronouns. Owen sits on the red couch. He snuggles his dog. He watches TV. Owen sits on the red couch, snuggling his dog and watching TV.	Have children break a sentence into its clauses. Each clause should have its own idea. Highlight each referential pronoun and replace it with the appropriate noun. Because they were far away from the king and angry about taxation, the colonists began to govern themselves. — Colonists began to govern themselves. — Because the colonists were far away from the king — And the colonists were angry about taxation

Apply. Read the passage aloud, have children read in pairs, or have them read quietly on their own. Prompt children to pause after complex sentences to break them apart and discuss the meaning. Then prompt them to highlight and draw arrows between pronouns and the nouns they refer to. After supported passage reading, send children to finish reading the text with a partner or independently.

The Girl With the Birthday That Disappears

My name is Pam. I am ten years old, and I have a birthday that most years forget.

So when friends ask, "When do you turn eleven?" I say, "I kind of don't—at least not this year." That's when they give me a weird look, like I'm joking. But I'm not. I was born on February 29th, which only shows up about every four years. I was born in a leap year, in other words.

This year is not a leap year. Today is March 1st. Yesterday was February 28th. So my birthday disappeared, and I guess I'm still ten. That's what I tell myself as I look at the calendar at school.

But when I get home, my mom says, "Happy birthday, Pam!" I tell her it's not my birthday.

Mom gives me a hug and says, "Let's play pretend!" What does she mean? She leads me into the dining room where Todd, Jim, and Jade, my best friends, greet me with a big "SURPRISE!" Then they sing "Happy Birthday to You." Mom brings in a big cake, with eleven lit candles on top, and says, "Make a wish!"

But I don't need to because I already got my wish: a birthday!

Prompt. Encourage students to make sense of complex syntax by following these guidelines.

- If a student does not understand the connection between two sentences, try direct questions or defining the connective: "How are these sentences connected? The connective *in contrast* means the next sentence might tell opposite information from the first sentence."
- If a student does not understand a referential pronoun, try making it visual: "Let's highlight the pronoun. Who or what is 'it'? We can highlight our other options by looking at the preceding sentences. Now, let's draw a line to the noun: *it* stands for the basket."
- If a student can't combine a sentence, try giving a conjunction: "Let's use the conjunction *after* to put these sentences together."
- If a student can't find the clauses to take apart, try reminding, "Each clause will tell us a different idea. Does this sentence have more than one idea?"

Progress Monitoring and Moving On

Complex syntax is, well, complex. For example, even children without difficulties may be confused by a sentence such as, "Dogs that have hair rather than fur tend to be hypoallergenic," through elementary school (Zipoli, 2017). Due to the overall lack of research on teaching syntactic skills, it is difficult to estimate how much support children will need. I recommend teaching complex syntactic structures before they come up in content-area texts. That will improve children's ability to understand those texts, thereby supporting comprehension and knowledge building. You might check a forthcoming chapter in an ELA book for complex syntactic structures and pre-teach them in small groups for children who are having difficulty with comprehension.

Changing the Rigor	Number of Clauses	How Clauses Are Combined
START HERE	2 clauses	*and, because*
INCREASE THE RIGOR	3+ clauses	*before, after*
... AND THEN		Relative pronouns (*who, which, that*)

8.3 How to Strengthen Understanding of Text Structure

Purpose: To support children in understanding a complex text by using its structure to identify its main idea.

Problem This Routine Solves

How many times have you asked, "So what was this book mostly about?" only to get nothing but silence? Perhaps the answer is, "More times than I can count." Students may struggle to make sense of texts for a variety of reasons, including because they do not know how to follow the organization of ideas. In other words, difficulties navigating the text's structure may get in the way of making sense of the text. When that happens, it is difficult for students to reach deep comprehension (Rapp et al., 2007).

Does this sound familiar?

Children who need support understanding complex text may:

- Blankly stare or flip through the book when asked to retell a text.
- Be able to summarize narrative texts but not expository/ informational texts.
- Answer questions such as, "What was the main idea?" by restating the title or saying something in the last part of what they read.
- Be able to identify main ideas and details in some text structures but not others.

This problem is most likely to occur when children are reading expository texts (Williams, 2018). Expository texts tend to be more complex than narrative texts and contain unfamiliar content. They also tend to include more challenging content, academic vocabulary, and formal language (Kucan & Beck, 1997). All that makes comprehension challenging, particularly for children learning English or with specific language or reading difficulties.

What the Research Says

Strong readers actively make meaning when they read, using a variety of strategies, including using a text's structure to organize ideas in their minds (Hagaman et al., 2016; Rapp et al., 2007). When readers can connect ideas from a text in a logical manner, it is easier to generate a main idea ("get the gist") and understand the text at a deeper level (Kendeou & Van Den Broek, 2007). Teaching children to identify and use the text's structure can improve their main idea statements, as well as their overall understanding of the text (Hebert et al., 2018; Al Otaiba et al., 2018; Pyle et al., 2017; Strong, 2020).

Routine (About 15 minutes)

Materials

- Reading passage
- Highlighters, pens, and writing paper
- Comprehension prompting guide

Review. Introduce the text by reviewing key content (vocabulary, prior knowledge) critical to understanding the text.

Teach. Teach children to notice how the text is structured by asking them questions and identifying signal words. Start by modeling how you think about a text's structure by saying: "I can ask myself questions to figure out if a text uses a sequence structure such as these: Does this text tell us information in order? Do I see words such as *first, next, then, last*?" These think-alouds model the metacognitive steps students need to take. Over time, children will also become more metacognitive, able to understand and describe their own thinking process (McDonald et al., 2021). Next, model writing a main idea statement (the "gist").

	Cause and Effect	Compare and Contrast	Problem and Solution	Simple Description	Sequence
Signal Words and Phrases	*cause, because, in order to, lead to, as a result of*	*instead of, however, compared to, unlike, similar to, different from*	*problem, solution, difficulty, issue, response, suggestion*	*for example, such as, looks like, in particular*	*first, then, next, last, before, after, from there, beforehand*
Questions to Ask to Identify Structure	What happened? What happened as a result?	How are the topics the same? How are they different?	What is the problem? What is the solution?	What is the author trying to tell or teach us?	How is the author putting information in order?
Get the Gist/Main Idea	The main cause is ___. The main effect is ___.	___ and ___ were compared on ___, ___, and ___.	The main problem is ___. The solution(s) is/are ___.	The topic is ___. The text describes ___.	First, ___ happened. Then, ___. Finally, ___.

Based on Hudson et al., 2021; Wijekumar et al., 2023

Practice. Read the text aloud, have children read in pairs, or have all group members read the text quietly and then join in a choral reading. When they're finished, have children identify the text structure by having them find signal words and asking them key questions.

Apply. After reading the text and identifying the text structure, have children generate a "get the gist" statement. Then have them extend the statement into a summary using key details or, if needed, inferences. See details after the Progress Monitoring and Moving On section.

Prompt. Support students as they discuss the gist and generate statements.

- If a student highlights words that are not signal words, try modeling: "Let's highlight some signal words together. The first sentence starts, 'A big issue in this community...' I'm going to highlight the word *issue* because it signals this text might be a problem-and-solution text."
- If a student identifies the wrong structure, try key questions: "You said this is a comparison text. In this text, what objects, concepts, or categories were compared?"

Extend the Lesson. Don't just leave kids hanging with the gist! After generating a statement and adding key details, help them make a connection to content-area instruction or prior knowledge. To transform their writing into a summary, guide children to the text's key details. You can also give them sentence starters connected to the text's structures.

Example: The problem was ______. The cause of the problem was ______. The solution was ______. The solution ______(did work / didn't work / fixed the problem by, etc.). (Hudson et al., 2021)

Progress Monitoring and Moving On

Using text structure to determine a text's main idea and summarize a text impacts readers' comprehension over time. Expect to teach at least two lessons a week over four weeks (Wijekumar et al., 2023) before seeing real results. Encourage students to continue using this strategy for retelling texts in situations beyond the small group.

Changing the Rigor	Passage Selection	Support
START HERE	Passages with a clear structure	Lead the entire routine with the small group.
INCREASE THE RIGOR	Passages with multiple structures or a less obvious structure	Remind children of their task and release them to read and write "get the gist" statements on their own.

8.4 How to Strengthen Generating Inferences

Purpose: To support children in using inference generation with explicit modeling, questioning, and integration of background knowledge.

Problem This Routine Solves

After reading this section of "Our Beautiful Town Is Gone" by Lauren Tarshis (Scholastic, 2019), you might ask students, "Why did Eleanor think she was dreaming?" Students may provide a range of responses, including "I don't know," "It was dark outside," or "She felt sleepy."

> "This can't be happening."
>
> That's what nine-year-old Eleanor Weddig was thinking as she sat in the car with her father. It was the morning of November 8, 2018, and Eleanor was caught in the middle of what would become the deadliest wildfire in the history of California. All across the town of Paradise, thousands of houses were in flames. Trees burned like giant torches. Ash fell from the sky. The morning sky was midnight dark.
>
> "Am I dreaming?" Eleanor kept asking herself. She pinched her leg, hard, trying to wake herself up.
>
> But Eleanor wasn't asleep.

Because information is not explicitly stated in a text, readers might fail to realize they need to make an inference, make inaccurate connections to background knowledge, or be unable to engage in the process of inference generation (Castles et al., 2018).

Does this sound familiar?

Students who need help with inference generation may:

- Accurately answer literal questions but struggle with "Why do you think...?" or "What can we learn...?"
- Make guesses based on personal opinions instead of the text.
- Struggle to use context to understand new words (Cain et al., 2004). See Routine 8.1 for a more specific routine for this!

What the Research Says

Understanding language, both in texts and conversations, requires inference generation. Readers make inferences by connecting explicitly stated information with ideas across texts and with background knowledge. While research finds that important aspects of inference generation happen automatically, readers can also use specific strategies to improve inference generation and comprehension (Cook & O'Brien, 2017). This is particularly important for readers who have difficulty comprehending texts: Struggling comprehenders tend to make fewer inferences than their peers, and this lack of inferencing may cause reading difficulties (Cain & Oakhill, 1999). Further, analyses of standardized reading assessments find that 50 to 90 percent of questions require inference generation, highlighting the importance of inference generation in comprehension (Rice et al., 2024).

Effective inference instruction includes:

- Modeling thinking aloud to link ideas across a text.
- Teaching strategies like identifying clue words or using graphic organizers.
- Scaffolded practice in multiple text types.
- Explicit feedback on whether students' inferences are text-supported (Rice et al., 2024).

Materials

- Reading passages
- Graphic organizer with three columns:

  What the Text Says
  What I Know
  What I Can Infer
- Prepared inference questions

Routine (About 15 minutes)

During your first lesson, use Routine 8.3 to generate a clear retell. This will ensure children are not confused by the basic ideas in the text before engaging in inference generation. During your second lesson, use this routine to focus on inferences.

Because inference generation requires integrating new information with background knowledge, it is critical to select passages from texts that are part of knowledge-building experiences. Select passages from ELA, science, or social studies texts that you're already reading or construct a text set with at least six topically connected texts for inference instruction.

Review. Reintroduce the text by reviewing key content (vocabulary, prior knowledge) critical to understanding the text or by sharing students' retells from the previous lesson. If reading "Our Beautiful Town Is Gone," you might say, "This passage is about a deadly wildfire. A wildfire is a big fire that spreads very quickly and is hard to stop. They are very dangerous when they come close to towns and cities. This is important to understand before we read." Then have students reread the passage.

Teach. Teach children how to make inferences by modeling your thinking within a graphic organizer. For example, you might model connecting ideas across a text and with prior knowledge: "How was this fire in Paradise different from other California fires? This question asks me about differences. I remember in the middle of reading this article, it said that fires are common but that this one was bigger and deadlier. It says that climate change has made fires hotter and less predictable. I can write this in 'What the Text Says.' I know that if a fire is hotter, it burns more and is more dangerous. I can write this in 'What I Know.' Together, I think the Paradise fire was different from other California fires because the changing climate made it hotter and faster, so it caused more devastation."

Practice. Ask a second inference question. Work with students to complete the organizer. Guide them to identify clue words related to the question.

Apply. Ask a third inference question. Have children discuss the question with a partner and fill out the graphic organizer on their own to answer. Be sure to give clear, explicit feedback.

Prompt. Support students in making inferences by thinking about feedback students need if they make an incorrect inference:

- If a student references irrelevant background knowledge, try focusing on relevant knowledge: "The question is about natural disasters. What have we learned in science about various natural disasters?"
- If a student references irrelevant information in the text, try asking: "What part of the text made you think that?" or "Can you prove your thinking with clues from the text?"

Progress Monitoring and Moving On

Inference instruction is most effective when paired with opportunities to build knowledge and vocabulary (Barth & Elleman, 2017; Rice & Wijekumar, 2024). Teaching children to fill out a graphic organizer is not the goal: The goal is to support children in integrating background knowledge with information explicitly stated in texts to build a more coherent understanding of the text. Like all aspects of language comprehension, there will not be a moment when children "move on" from inference generation, but this routine may help you bolster children's skills.

Connect whole-group and small-group lessons by using the same language and graphic organizers to support inference generation over time.

Changing the Rigor	Type of Inference Questions	Text Genre	Strategies
START HERE	Text-based ("Why did ___ happen?")	Narrative texts	Questioning
INCREASE THE RIGOR	Knowledge-based ("What lesson can we learn?")	Expository or informational texts	Graphic organizers

In Closing, Remember This Swap...

Less comprehension instruction with unconnected texts → More targeted practice to improve access to content-area texts.

Teaching children to comprehend complex texts is no easy feat. There is one central goal that makes this instruction more manageable and meaningful: building children's knowledge. It may seem like a better idea to focus on mastering comprehension strategies. But teaching strategies only support comprehension when paired with building children's knowledge (Peng et al., 2024). Centering knowledge ensures instruction is authentic, purposeful, and engaging.

As I've mentioned, the routines in this chapter are not the only ingredients in supporting language comprehension with complex texts. Use these as a framework for thinking differently about small-group instruction by asking yourself: What is making texts hard for this student? What about this particular text is hard? Then target practice in small-group instruction to build proficiency and improve access to grade-level texts. If you aren't sure where to start, most children will benefit from Routine 8.3, identifying a text's structure and using it to frame a summary. You can even use it during whole-class instruction to support everyone's comprehension more efficiently.

Conclusion

Teaching children to read requires enormous expertise, as well as the right instruction, materials, and support. To ensure all children become proficient, empowered readers, we need to use every tool in our research-based toolbox. With that in mind, I want to leave you with two final thoughts:

If you see something, teach something. This book focuses on specific, research-based routines in word recognition, fluency, and comprehension that can help you solve specific challenges children encounter in reading. If a student is stuck trying to decode multisyllabic words, we don't have to cross our fingers and hope. We can use clear routines to give more explicit instruction, more practice, and more feedback.

Use small-group instruction to build a community of readers. When we meet with smaller groups of children, we have the opportunity to create connections. Smaller groups help you get to know your students better than only whole-class instruction. Smaller groups allow some students to feel more comfortable making mistakes, building trust and respect with their peers. Smaller groups allow readers more time with interesting texts and topics. In other words, small-group instruction not only contributes to children's skills but also to building more motivated, engaged readers.

Julia

References

Al Otaiba, S., Allor, J. H., Baker, K., Conner, C., Stewart, J., & Mellado de la Cruz, V. M. (2019). Teaching phonemic awareness and word reading skills: Focusing on explicit and systematic approaches. *Perspectives on Language and Literacy, 45*, 11–16.

Al Otaiba, S., Connor, C. M., & Crowe, E. (2018). Promise and feasibility of teaching expository text structure: A primary grade pilot study. *Reading and Writing, 31*(9), 1997–2015.

Al Otaiba, S., Connor, C. M., Folsom, J. S., Greulich, L., Meadows, J., & Li, Z. (2011). Assessment data-informed guidance to individualized kindergarten reading instruction: Findings from a cluster-randomized control field trial. *The Elementary School Journal, 111*(4), 535–560.

Al Otaiba, S., McMaster, K., Wanzek, J., & Zaru, M. W. (2023). What we know and need to know about literacy interventions for elementary students with reading difficulties and disabilities, including dyslexia. *Reading Research Quarterly, 58*(2), 313–332.

Anderson, R. C., & Nagy, W. E. (1993). The vocabulary conundrum. *Center for the Study of Reading Technical Report*, no. 570.

Archer, A. L., Gleason, M. M., & Vachon, V. L. (2003). Decoding and fluency: Foundation skills for struggling older readers. *Learning Disability Quarterly, 26*(2), 89–101.

Aspiranti, K. B., Reynolds, J. L., Henze, E. E., Grekov, P., & Martinez, J. C. (2024). An analysis of word/sound boxes and their effects on basic literacy skills. *Education and Treatment of Children, 47*(3), 271–283.

Austin, C. R., Vaughn, S., Clemens, N. H., Pustejovsky, J. E., & Boucher, A. N. (2022). The relative effects of instruction linking word reading and word meaning compared to word reading instruction alone on the accuracy, fluency, and word meaning knowledge of 4th–5th grade students with dyslexia. *Scientific Studies of Reading, 26*(3), 204–222.

Austin, C., Stevens, L., Demchack, A., & Solari, E. (2023). Orton Gillingham: Which aspects are supported by research and which require additional research. *The Reading League Journal, 4*(3), 5–15.

Babayiğit, S. (2014). The role of oral language skills in reading and listening comprehension of text: A comparison of monolingual (L1) and bilingual (L2) speakers of English language. *Journal of Research in Reading, 37*(S1), S22–S47.

Baker, D. L., Burns, D., Kame'enui, E. J., Smolkowski, K., & Baker, S. K. (2016). Does supplemental instruction support the transition from Spanish to English reading instruction for first-grade English learners at risk of reading difficulties? *Learning Disability Quarterly, 39*(4), 226–239.

Ball, E. W., & Blachman, B. A. (1991). Does phoneme awareness training in kindergarten make a difference in early word recognition and developmental spelling? *Reading Research Quarterly, 26*(1), 49–66.

Barth, A. E., & Elleman, A. (2017). Evaluating the impact of a multi-strategy inference intervention for middle-grade struggling readers. *Language, Speech, and Hearing Services in Schools, 48*(1), 31–41.

Baye, A., Slavin, R. E., Lake, C., Inns, A., & Haslam, J. (2019). *Reading programmes for secondary students: Evidence review*. Education Endowment Foundation.

Beck, I. L., & Beck, M. E. (2013). *Making sense of phonics*. Guilford Press.

Beck, I. L., & McKeown, M. G. (2007). Increasing young low-income children's oral vocabulary repertoires through rich and focused instruction. *The Elementary School Journal, 107*(3), 251–271.

Becker, R., & Sylvan, L. (2021). Coupling articulatory placement strategies with phonemic awareness instruction to support emergent literacy skills in preschool children: A collaborative approach. *Language, Speech, and Hearing Services in Schools, 52*(2), 661–674.

Begeny, J. C., Levy, R. A., & Field, S. A. (2018). Using small-group instruction to improve students' reading fluency: An evaluation of the existing research. *Journal of Applied School Psychology, 34*(1), 36–64.

Benjamin, R. G., & Schwanenflugel, P. J. (2010). Text complexity and oral reading prosody in young readers. *Reading Research Quarterly, 45*(4), 388–404.

Berninger, V. W., Rutberg, J. E., Abbott, R. D., Garcia, N., Anderson-Youngstrom, M., Brooks, A., & Fulton, C. (2006). Tier 1 and Tier 2 early intervention for handwriting and composing. *Journal of School Psychology, 44*(1), 3–30.

Bhattacharya, A., & Ehri, L. C. (2004). Graphosyllabic analysis helps adolescent struggling readers read and spell words. *Journal of Learning Disabilities, 37*(4), 331–348.

Bigozzi, L., Tarchi, C., Vagnoli, L., Valente, E., & Pinto, G. (2017). Reading fluency as a predictor of school outcomes across grades 4–9. *Frontiers in Psychology, 8*, 200.

Bonneton-Botté, N., Miramand, L., Bailly, R., & Pons, C. (2023). Teaching and rehabilitation of handwriting for children in the digital age: Issues and challenges. *Children, 10*(7), 1096.

Bowers, J. S., & Bowers, P. N. (2018). Progress in reading instruction requires a better understanding of the English spelling system. *Current Directions in Psychological Science, 27*(6), 407–412.

Bowey, J. A., & Muller, D. (2005). Phonological recoding and rapid orthographic learning in third-graders' silent reading: A critical test of the self-teaching hypothesis. *Journal of Experimental Child Psychology, 92*(3), 203–219.

Boyer, N., & Ehri, L. C. (2011). Contribution of phonemic segmentation instruction with letters and articulation pictures to word reading and spelling in beginners. *Scientific Studies of Reading, 15*(5), 440–470.

Brysbaert, M., Stevens, M., Mandera, P., & Keuleers, E. (2016). How many words do we know? Practical estimates of vocabulary size dependent on word definition, the degree of language input and the participant's age. *Frontiers in Psychology, 7*, 1116.

Burns, M. K. (2024). Assessing an instructional level during reading fluency interventions: A meta-analysis of the effects on reading. *Assessment for Effective Intervention, 49*(4), 214–224.

Burns, M. K., Dean, V. J., & Foley, S. (2004). Preteaching unknown key words with incremental rehearsal to improve reading fluency and comprehension with children identified as reading disabled. *Journal of School Psychology, 42*(4), 303–314.

Burns, M. K., Duesenberg-Marshall, M. D., McCollom, E. M., McCree, N., & Abdelnaby, H. Z. (2022). Preteaching words to facilitate an instructional level in reading with a student with a specific learning disability in reading. *Learning Disabilities: A Multidisciplinary Journal, 27*(1).

Burns, M. K., Duesenberg-Marshall, M. D., & Romero, M. E. (2024). Effects of a classwide reading intervention on reading fluency and comprehension of content area text with students in middle school. *The Journal of Educational Research, 117*(6), 378–386.

Burns, M. K., Duke, N. K., & Cartwright, K. B. (2023). Evaluating components of the active view of reading as intervention targets: Implications for social justice. *School Psychology, 38*(1), 30.

Burns, M. K., Pulles, S. M., Maki, K. E., Kanive, R., Hodgson, J., Helman, L. A., & Preast, J. L. (2015). Accuracy of student performance while reading leveled books rated at their instructional level by a reading inventory. *Journal of School Psychology, 53*(6), 437–445.

Cain, K., & Oakhill, J. V. (1999). Inference making ability and its relation to comprehension failure in young children. *Reading and Writing, 11*(5), 489–503.

Cain, K., Oakhill, J. V., Barnes, M. A., & Bryant, P. E. (2001). Comprehension skill, inference-making ability, and their relation to knowledge. *Memory & Cognition, 29*(6), 850–859.

Cain, K., Oakhill, J., & Lemmon, K. (2004). Individual differences in the inference of word meanings from context: The influence of reading comprehension, vocabulary knowledge, and memory capacity. *Journal of Educational Psychology, 96*(4), 671.

Caravolas, M., Lervåg, A., Mikulajová, M., Defior, S., Seidlová-Málková, G., & Hulme, C. (2019). A cross-linguistic, longitudinal study of the foundations of decoding and reading comprehension ability. *Scientific Studies of Reading, 23*(5), 386–402.

Cárdenas-Hagan, E. (2020). *Literacy foundations for English learners: A comprehensive guide to evidence-based instruction*. Brookes Publishing Company.

Castiglioni-Spalten, M. L., & Ehri, L. C. (2003). Phonemic awareness instruction: Contribution of articulatory segmentation to novice beginners' reading and spelling. *Scientific Studies of Reading, 7*(1), 25–52.

Castle, S., Deniz, C. B., & Tortora, M. (2005). Flexible grouping and student learning in a high-needs school. *Education and Urban Society, 37*(2), 139–150.

Castles, A., Rastle, K., & Nation, K. (2018). Ending the reading wars: Reading acquisition from novice to expert. *Psychological Science in the Public Interest, 19*(1), 5–51.

Cervetti, G. N., Fitzgerald, M. S., Hiebert, E. H., & Hebert, M. (2023). Meta-analysis examining the impact of vocabulary instruction on vocabulary knowledge and skill. *Reading Psychology, 44*(6), 672–709.

Cervetti, G. N., Wright, T. S., & Hwang, H. (2016). Conceptual coherence, comprehension, and vocabulary acquisition: A knowledge effect? *Reading and Writing, 29*(4), 761–779.

Cheatham, J. P., Allor, J. H., & Roberts, J. K. (2014). How does independent practice of multiple-criteria text influence the reading performance and development of second graders? *Learning Disability Quarterly, 37*(1), 3–14.

Cho, E., Capin, P., Roberts, G., Roberts, G. J., & Vaughn, S. (2019). Examining sources and mechanisms of reading comprehension difficulties: Comparing English learners and non-English learners within the simple view of reading. *Journal of Educational Psychology, 111*(6), 982.

Chu, M. C., & Chen, S. H. (2014). Comparison of the effects of two phonics training programs on L2 word reading. *Psychological Reports, 114*(1), 272–291.

Clark, R., Morrison, T. G., & Wilcox, B. (2009). Readers' theater: A process of developing fourth-graders' reading fluency. *Reading Psychology, 30*(4), 359–385.

Colenbrander, D., Kohnen, S., Beyersmann, E., Robidoux, S., Wegener, S., Arrow, T., & Castles, A. (2022). Teaching children to read irregular words: A comparison of three instructional methods. *Scientific Studies of Reading, 26*(6), 545–564.

Colenbrander, D., von Hagen, A., Kohnen, S., Wegener, S., Ko, K., Beyersmann, E., & Castles, A. (2024). The effects of morphological instruction on literacy outcomes for children in English-speaking countries: A systematic review and meta-analysis. *Educational Psychology Review, 36*(4), 119.

Connor, C. M. (2014). Individualizing teaching in beginning reading. *Better: Evidence-Based Education*, Autumn, 4–7.

Connor, C. M., & Morrison, F. J. (2016). Individualizing student instruction in reading: Implications for policy and practice. *Policy Insights from the Behavioral and Brain Sciences, 3*(1), 54–61.

Connor, C. M., Alberto, P. A., Compton, D. L., & O'Connor, R. E. (2014). *Improving reading outcomes for students with or at risk for reading disabilities: A synthesis of the contributions from the Institute of Education Sciences Research Centers*. NCSER 2014–3000. National Center for Special Education Research.

Connor, C. M., Morrison, F. J., Fishman, B., Crowe, E. C., Al Otaiba, S., & Schatschneider, C. (2013). A longitudinal cluster-randomized controlled study on the accumulating effects of individualized literacy instruction on students' reading from first through third grade. *Psychological Science, 24*(8), 1408–1419.

Connor, C. M., Morrison, F. J., Schatschneider, C., Toste, J. R., Lundblom, E., Crowe, E. C., & Fishman, B. (2011). Effective classroom instruction: Implications of child characteristics by reading instruction interactions on first graders' word reading achievement. *Journal of Research on Educational Effectiveness, 4*(3), 173–207.

Connor, C. M., Piasta, S. B., Fishman, B., Glasney, S., Schatschneider, C., Crowe, E., Underwood, P., & Morrison, F. J. (2009). Individualizing student instruction precisely: Effects of child instruction interactions on first graders' literacy development. *Child Development, 80*(1), 77–100.

Conrad, N. J., Kennedy, K., Saoud, W., Scallion, L., & Hanusiak, L. (2019). Establishing word representations through reading and spelling: Comparing degree of orthographic learning. *Journal of Research in Reading, 42*(1), 162–177.

Conradi Smith, K., Amendum, S. J., & Williams, T. W. (2022). Maximizing small-group reading instruction. *Reading Teacher, 76*(3), 348–356.

Constable, C. M. (2010). *A comparison of continuous versus segmented speech production in teaching decoding and spelling to children at risk for reading difficulty*. City University of New York.

Cook, A. E., & O'Brien, E. J. (2017). Fundamentals of inferencing during reading. *Language and Linguistics Compass, 11*(7).

Crosson, A. C., & Lesaux, N. K. (2013). Connectives: Fitting another piece of the vocabulary instruction puzzle. *The Reading Teacher, 67*(3), 193–200.

Cunningham, P. M., & Cunningham, J. W. (1992). Making words: Enhancing the invented spelling-decoding connection. *The Reading Teacher, 46*(2), 106–115.

Deacon, S. H., & Kieffer, M. (2018). Understanding how syntactic awareness contributes to reading comprehension: Evidence from mediation and longitudinal models. *Journal of Educational Psychology, 110*(1), 72.

Downs, J., & Mohr, K. A. (2025). A multilevel meta-analysis of synchronous paired oral reading techniques in elementary classrooms. *Literacy Research and Instruction, 64*(1), 84–111.

Duke, N. K. (2020). When readers get stuck: There's an art—and science—to providing prompts for young readers when they struggle. *Educational Leadership, 78*(3), 26–33.

Duke, N. K., & Cartwright, K. B. (2021). The science of reading progresses: Communicating advances beyond the simple view of reading. *Reading Research Quarterly, 56,* S25–S44.

Duke, N. K., Ward, A. E., & Pearson, P. D. (2021). The science of reading comprehension instruction. *The Reading Teacher, 74*(6), 663–672.

Dussling, T. (2020). English language learners and native English-speakers' spelling growth after supplemental early reading instruction. *International Journal of Education and Literacy Studies, 8*(1), 1–7.

Dyson, H., Best, W., Solity, J., & Hulme, C. (2017). Training mispronunciation correction and word meanings improves children's ability to learn to read words. *Scientific Studies of Reading, 21*(5), 392–407.

Edwards, A. A., Steacy, L. M., Rigobon, V. M., Siegelman, N., Rueckl, J. G., & Compton, D. L. (2025). Is the role of set for variability in word reading influenced by conditions leading to partial decoding? *Scientific Studies of Reading,* 1–15.

Ehlert, M., Beck, J., Förster, N., & Souvignier, E. (2025). Continuous texts or word lists? Exploring the effects and the process of repeated reading depending on the reading material and students' reading abilities. *Reading and Writing, 38*(3), 745–764.

Ehri, L. C. (1995). Phases of development in learning to read words by sight. *Journal of Research in Reading, 18*(2), 116–125.

Ehri, L. C. (2014). Orthographic mapping in the acquisition of sight word reading, spelling memory, and vocabulary learning. *Scientific Studies of Reading, 18*(1), 5–21.

Ehri, L. C. (2017). Reconceptualizing the development of sight word reading and its relationship to recoding. In *Reading acquisition* (pp. 107–143). Routledge.

Elbro, C., de Jong, P. F., Houter, D., & Nielsen, A. M. (2012). From spelling pronunciation to lexical access: A second step in word decoding? *Scientific Studies of Reading, 16*(4), 341–359.

Erbeli, F., & Rice, M. (2022). Examining the effects of silent independent reading on reading outcomes: A narrative synthesis review from 2000 to 2020. *Reading & Writing Quarterly, 38*(3), 253–271.

Erbeli, F., Rice, M., Xu, Y., Bishop, M. E., & Goodrich, J. M. (2024). A meta-analysis on the optimal cumulative dosage of early phonemic awareness instruction. *Scientific Studies of Reading, 28*(4), 345–370.

Erekson, J. A. (2010). Prosody and interpretation. *Reading Horizons: A Journal of Literacy and Language Arts, 50*(2), 3.

Faggella-Luby, M., & Wardwell, M. (2011). RTI in a middle school: Findings and practical implications of a Tier 2 reading comprehension study. *Learning Disability Quarterly, 34*(1), 35–49.

Fien, H., Smith, J. L., Smolkowski, K., Baker, S. K., Nelson, N. J., & Chaparro, E. (2015). An examination of the efficacy of a multitiered intervention on early reading outcomes for first grade students at risk for reading difficulties. *Journal of Learning Disabilities, 48*(6), 602–621.

Filderman, M. J., & Toste, J. R. (2022). Effects of varying levels of data use to intensify a multisyllabic word reading intervention for upper elementary students with or at risk for reading disabilities. *Journal of Learning Disabilities, 55*(5), 393–407.

Firmender, J. M., Reis, S. M., & Sweeny, S. M. (2013). Reading comprehension and fluency levels ranges across diverse classrooms: The need for differentiated reading instruction and content. *Gifted Child Quarterly, 57*(1), 3–14.

Fisher, D., & Frey, N. (2014). Close reading as an intervention for struggling middle school readers. *Journal of Adolescent & Adult Literacy, 57*(5), 367–376.

Fitzgerald, L. R., Libnoch, H. A., Park, S., & Piasta, S. B. (2020). Best practices in alphabet instruction: Lessons (version 2). Crane Center for Early Childhood Research and Policy, The Ohio State University.

Fulmer, S. M., & Frijters, J. C. (2011). Motivation during an excessively challenging reading task: The buffering role of relative topic interest. *The Journal of Experimental Education, 79*(2), 185–208.

Garrett, T. D., & O'Connor, D. (2010). Readers' theater: "Hold on, let's read it again." *Teaching Exceptional Children, 43*(1), 6–13.

Gellert, A. S., Arnbak, E., Wischmann, S., & Elbro, C. (2021). Morphological intervention for students with limited vocabulary knowledge: Short- and long-term transfer effects. *Reading Research Quarterly, 56*(3), 583–601.

Gersten, R., Baker, S. K., Shanahan, T., Linan-Thompson, S., Collins, P., & Scarcella, R. (2007). Effective Literacy and English Language Instruction for English Learners in the Elementary Grades. IES Practice Guide. NCEE 2007-4011. National Center for Education Evaluation and Regional Assistance, Institute of Education Sciences, U.S. Department of Education.

Goldenberg, C. (2020). Reading wars, reading science, and English learners. *Reading Research Quarterly, 55,* S131–S144.

Gonzalez-Frey, S. M., & Ehri, L. C. (2021). Connected phonation is more effective than segmented phonation for teaching beginning readers to decode unfamiliar words. *Scientific Studies of Reading, 25*(3), 272–285.

Goodwin, A. P., Huggins, A. C., Carlo, M. S., August, D., & Calderon, M. (2013). Minding morphology: How morphological awareness relates to reading for English language learners. *Reading and Writing, 26*(9), 1387–1415.

Gough, P. B., & Tunmer, W. E. (1986). Decoding, reading, and reading disability. *Remedial and Special Education, 7*(1), 6–10.

Graesser, A. C., McNamara, D. S., Cai, Z., Conley, M., Li, H., & Pennebaker, J. (2014). Coh-Metrix measures text characteristics at multiple levels of language and discourse. *The Elementary School Journal, 115*(2), 210–229.

Graham, S. (1999). Handwriting and spelling instruction for students with learning disabilities: A review. *Learning Disability Quarterly, 22*(2), 78–98.

Graham, S., & Harris, K. R. (2018). Evidence-based writing practices: A meta-analysis of existing meta-analyses. *Design Principles for Teaching Effective Writing, 34,* 13–37.

Graham, S., & Hebert, M. (2010). *Writing to read: Evidence for how writing can improve reading*. A report from Carnegie Corporation of New York.

Graham, S., & Perin, D. (2007). A meta-analysis of writing instruction for adolescent students. *Journal of Educational Psychology, 99*(3), 445.

Graham, S., Harris, K. R., & Adkins, M. (2018). The impact of supplemental handwriting and spelling instruction with first grade students who do not acquire transcription skills as rapidly as peers: A randomized control trial. *Reading and Writing, 31*(6), 1273–1294.

Green, C., Keogh, K., & Prout, J. (2024). The CPB sight words: A new research-based high-frequency wordlist for early reading instruction. *The Reading Teacher, 78*(1), 56–64.

Hagaman, J. L., Casey, K. J., & Reid, R. (2016). Paraphrasing strategy instruction for struggling readers. *Preventing School Failure: Alternative Education for Children and Youth, 60*(1), 43–52.

Hall, C., Dahl-Leonard, K., Cho, E., Solari, E. J., Capin, P., Conner, C. L., & Kehoe, K. F. (2023). Forty years of reading intervention research for elementary students with or at risk for dyslexia: A systematic review and meta-analysis. *Reading Research Quarterly, 58*(2), 285–312.

Hall, C., Vaughn, S., Barnes, M. A., Stewart, A. A., Austin, C. R., & Roberts, G. (2020). The effects of inference instruction on the reading comprehension of English learners with reading comprehension difficulties. *Remedial and Special Education, 41*(5), 259–270.

Hall, M. S., & Burns, M. K. (2018). Meta-analysis of targeted small-group reading interventions. *Journal of School Psychology, 66,* 54–66.

Hammerschmidt-Snidarich, S. M., Maki, K. E., & Adams, S. R. (2019). Evaluating the effects of repeated reading and continuous reading using a standardized dosage of words read. *Psychology in the Schools, 56*(5), 635–651.

Harn, B. A., Linan-Thompson, S., & Roberts, G. (2008). Intensifying instruction: Does additional instructional time make a difference for the most at-risk first graders? *Journal of Learning Disabilities, 41*(2), 115–125.

Hassler, K. M., Cook, S. E., & Meng, P. M. (2025). Fostering reading success: Investigating connected phonation as a key strategy for word reading fluency. *Reading & Writing Quarterly*, 1–14.

Hatcher, P. J., & Hulme, C. (1999). Phonemes, rhymes, and intelligence as predictors of children's responsiveness to remedial reading instruction: Evidence from a longitudinal intervention study. *Journal of Experimental Child Psychology, 72*(2), 130–153.

Hatcher, P. J., Hulme, C., Miles, J. N. V., Carroll, J. M., Hatcher, J., Gibbs, S., Smith, G., Bowyer-Crane, C., & Snowling, M. J. (2005). Efficacy of small group reading intervention for beginning readers with reading-delay: A randomized controlled trial: Efficacy of small group reading intervention. *Journal of Child Psychology and Psychiatry, 47*(8), 820–827.

Hattie, J., & Timperley, H. (2007). The power of feedback. *Review of Educational Research, 77*(1), 81–112.

Hebert, M., Bohaty, J. J., Nelson, J. R., & Lambert, M. C. (2018). Identifying and discriminating expository text structures: An experiment with 4th and 5th grade struggling readers. *Reading and Writing, 31*(9), 2115–2145.

Heggie, L., & Wade-Woolley, L. (2017). Reading longer words: Insights into multisyllabic word reading. *Perspectives of the ASHA Special Interest Groups, 2*(1), 86–94.

Hiebert, E. H. (2017). The texts of literacy instruction: Obstacles to or opportunities for educational equity? *Literacy Research: Theory, Method, and Practice, 66*(1), 117–134.

Hudson, A. K., Owens, J., Moore, K. A., Lambright, K., & Wijekumar, K. (2021). "What's the main idea?" Using text structure to build comprehension. *The Reading Teacher, 75*(1), 113–118.

Hudson, A., Koh, P. W., Moore, K. A., & Binks-Cantrell, E. (2020). Fluency interventions for elementary students with reading difficulties: A synthesis of research from 2000–2019. *Education Sciences, 10*(3), 52.

Hulme, C., & Snowling, M. J. (2013). Learning to read: What we know and what we need to understand better. *Child Development Perspectives, 7*(1), 1–5.

Hwang, H., Cabell, S. Q., & Joyner, R. E. (2023). Does cultivating content knowledge during literacy instruction support vocabulary and comprehension in the elementary school years? A systematic review. *Reading Psychology, 44*(2), 145–174.

Hwang, H., McMaster, K. L., & Kendeou, P. (2023). A longitudinal investigation of directional relations between domain knowledge and reading in the elementary years. *Reading Research Quarterly, 58*(1), 59–77.

Johns, J. L., & Wilke, K. H. (2018). High-frequency words: Some ways to teach and help students practice and learn them. *Texas Journal of Literacy Education, 6*(1), 3–13.

Jones, C. D., Clark, S. K., & Reutzel, D. R. (2013). Enhancing alphabet knowledge instruction: Research implications and practical strategies for early childhood educators. *Early Childhood Education Journal, 41*(2), 81–89.

Joseph, L. M. (2002). Facilitating word recognition and spelling using word boxes and word sort phonic procedures. *School Psychology Review, 31*(1), 122–129.

Juel, C., & Roper-Schneider, D. (1985). The influence of basal readers on first grade reading. *Reading Research Quarterly,* 134–152.

Kamps, D., Abbott, M., Greenwood, C., Wills, H., Veerkamp, M., & Kaufman, J. (2008). Effects of small-group reading instruction and curriculum differences for students most at risk in kindergarten: Two-year results for secondary- and tertiary-level interventions. *Journal of Learning Disabilities, 41*(2), 101–114.

Karemaker, A., Jelley, F., Clancy, C., & Sylva, K. (2017). The effects on children's literacy skills of reading e-books with different features: Are 'bells and whistles' over-rated? *International Journal of Child-Computer Interaction, 12,* 30–36.

Kearns, D. M. (2015). How elementary-age children read polysyllabic polymorphemic words. *Journal of Educational Psychology, 107*(2), 364.

Kearns, D. M. (2020). Does English have useful syllable division patterns? *Reading Research Quarterly, 55,* S145–S160.

Kearns, D. M., & Hiebert, E. H. (2022). The word complexity of primary-level texts: Differences between first and third grade in widely used curricula. *Reading Research Quarterly, 57*(1), 255–285.

Kearns, D. M., & Whaley, V. M. (2019). Helping students with dyslexia read long words: Using syllables and morphemes. *Teaching Exceptional Children, 51*(3), 212–225.

Keehn, S., Harmon, J., & Shoho, A. (2008). A study of readers theater in eighth grade: Issues of fluency, comprehension, and vocabulary. *Reading & Writing Quarterly, 24*(4), 335–362.

Kendeou, P., & Van Den Broek, P. (2007). The effects of prior knowledge and text structure on comprehension processes during reading of scientific texts. *Memory & Cognition, 35*(7), 1567–1577.

Kim, Y. S. G., & Zagata, E. (2024). Enhancing reading and writing skills through systematically integrated instruction. *The Reading Teacher, 77*(6), 787–799.

Kim, Y. S. G., Quinn, J. M., & Petscher, Y. (2021). What is text reading fluency and is it a predictor or an outcome of reading comprehension? A longitudinal investigation. *Developmental Psychology, 57*(5), 718.

Klingbeil, D. A., Nelson, P. M., Van Norman, E. R., & Birr, C. (2017). Diagnostic accuracy of multivariate universal screening procedures for reading in upper elementary grades. *Remedial and Special Education, 38*(5), 308–320.

Kucan, L., & Beck, I. L. (1997). Thinking aloud and reading comprehension research: Inquiry, instruction, and social interaction. *Review of Educational Research, 67*(3), 271–299.

Kuhn, M. R. (2020). Whole class or small group fluency instruction: A tutorial of four effective approaches. *Education Sciences, 10*(5), 145.

Kuhn, M. R., & Stahl, S. A. (2003). Fluency: A review of developmental and remedial practices. *Journal of Educational Psychology, 95*(1), 3.

Kulik, J. A., & Kulik, C. L. C. (1988). Timing of feedback and verbal learning. *Review of Educational Research, 58*(1), 79–97.

Kulik, J. A., & Kulik, C. L. C. (1992). Meta-analytic findings on grouping programs. *Gifted Child Quarterly, 36*(2), 73–77.

Kurtz, H., Lloyd, S., Harwin, A., Chen, V., Furuya, Y., EdWeek Research Center, & Education Writers Association. (2020). Early reading instruction results of a national survey of K–2 and elementary special education teachers and postsecondary instructors. In *Education Week*. Editorial Projects in Education Inc.

LaBerge, D., & Samuels, S. J. (1974). Toward a theory of automatic information processing in reading. *Cognitive Psychology, 6*(2), 293–323.

Lane, H. B., Contesse, V. A., Gage, N. A., & Burns, M. K. (2025). Effect of an instructional program in foundational reading skills on early literacy development of students in kindergarten and first grade. *Reading Research Quarterly, 60*(1).

Larabee, K. M., Burns, M. K., & McComas, J. J. (2014). Effects of an iPad-supported phonics intervention on decoding performance and time on-task. *Journal of Behavioral Education, 23,* 449–469.

Lenski, S., Larson, M., McElhone, D., Davis, D. S., Lauritzen, C., Villagómez, A., & Scales, W. D. (2016). What teachers want: A statewide survey of reading and English language arts teachers' instructional materials, preferences, and practices. *Literacy Research and Instruction, 55*(3), 237–261.

Lesaux, N. K., Crosson, A. C., Kieffer, M. J., & Pierce, M. (2010). Uneven profiles: Language minority learners' word reading, vocabulary, and reading comprehension skills. *Journal of Applied Developmental Psychology, 31*(6), 475–483.

Levasseur, V. M., Macaruso, P., Palumbo, L. C., & Shankweiler, D. (2006). Syntactically cued text facilitates oral reading fluency in developing readers. *Applied Psycholinguistics, 27*(3), 423–445.

Levesque, K. C., Breadmore, H. L., & Deacon, S. H. (2021). How morphology impacts reading and spelling: Advancing the role of morphology in models of literacy development. *Journal of Research in Reading, 44*(1), 10–26.

Levesque, K. C., Kieffer, M. J., & Deacon, S. H. (2019). Inferring meaning from meaningful parts: The contributions of morphological skills to the development of children's reading comprehension. *Reading Research Quarterly, 54*(1), 63–80.

Lindsey, J. B. (2022). *Reading above the fray: Reliable, research-based routines for developing decoding skills.* Scholastic.

Lopez-Escribano, C., Martin-Babarro, J., & Perez-Lopez, R. (2022). Promoting handwriting fluency for preschool and elementary-age students: Meta-analysis and meta-synthesis of research from 2000 to 2020. *Frontiers in Psychology, 13,* 841573.

Lou, Y., Abrami, P. C., Spence, J. C., Poulsen, C., Chambers, B., & d'Apollonia, S. (1996). Within-class grouping: A meta-analysis. *Review of Educational Research, 66*(4), 423–458.

Lovett, M. W., Lacerenza, L., Borden, S. L., Frijters, J. C., Steinbach, K. A., & De Palma, M. (2000). Components of effective remediation for developmental reading disabilities: Combining phonological and strategy-based instruction to improve outcomes. *Journal of Educational Psychology, 92,* 263–283.

Lovett, M. W., Lacerenza, L., Steinbach, K. A., & De Palma, M. (2014). Development and evaluation of a research-based intervention program for children and adolescents with reading disabilities. *Perspectives on Language and Literacy, 40*(3), 21–31.

MacKay, E., Lynch, E., Sorenson Duncan, T., & Deacon, S. H. (2021). Informing the science of reading: Students' awareness of sentence-level information is important for reading comprehension. *Reading Research Quarterly, 56,* S221–S230.

Maddox, K., & Feng, J. (2013). Whole language instruction vs. phonics instruction: Effect on reading fluency and spelling accuracy of first grade students. Online Submission.

Maki, K. E., & Hammerschmidt-Snidarich, S. (2022). Reading fluency intervention dosage: A novel meta-analysis and research synthesis. *Journal of School Psychology, 92,* 148–165.

Mastrothanasis, K., Kladaki, M., & Andreou, A. (2023). A systematic review and meta-analysis of the Readers' Theatre impact on the development of reading skills. *International Journal of Educational Research Open,* 4.

Mathwin, K. P., Chapparo, C., & Hinnit, J. (2022). Children with handwriting difficulties: Developing orthographic knowledge of alphabet-letters to improve capacity to write alphabet symbols. *Reading and Writing, 35*(4), 919–942.

McCandliss, B., Beck, I. L., Sandak, R., & Perfetti, C. (2003). Focusing attention on decoding for children with poor reading skills: Design and preliminary tests of the word building intervention. *Scientific Studies of Reading, 7*(1), 75–104.

McCarroll, H., & Fletcher, T. (2017). Does handwriting instruction have a place in the instructional day? The relationship between handwriting quality and academic success. *Cogent Education, 4*(1), 1386427.

McDonald, A., Morrison, T. G., Wilcox, B., & Billen, M. T. (2021). Improving children's reading comprehension by teaching inferences. *Reading Psychology, 42*(3), 264–280.

McKenna, M. C., Walpole, S., & Jang, B. G. (2017). Validation of the informal decoding inventory. *Assessment for Effective Intervention, 42*(2), 110–118.

McMaster, K. L., Fuchs, D., & Fuchs, L. S. (2006). Research on peer-assisted learning strategies: The promise and limitations of peer-mediated instruction. *Reading & Writing Quarterly, 22*(1), 5–25.

Mesmer, H. A. E. (2005). Text decodability and the first-grade reader. *Reading & Writing Quarterly, 21*(1), 61–86.

Mesmer, H. A. E. (2009). Textual scaffolds for developing fluency in beginning readers: Accuracy and reading rate in qualitatively leveled and decodable text. *Literacy Research and Instruction, 49*(1), 20–39.

Mesmer, H. A. (2024). *Big words for young readers: Teaching kids in grades K to 5 to decode—and understand—words with multiple syllables and morphemes*. Scholastic.

Miles, K. P., Rubin, G. B., & Gonzalez-Frey, S. (2018). Rethinking sight words. *The Reading Teacher, 71*(6), 715–726.

Miller, J., & Schwanenflugel, P. J. (2008). A longitudinal study of the development of reading prosody as a dimension of oral reading fluency in early elementary school children. *Reading Research Quarterly, 43*(4), 336–354.

Moats, L. C. (2004). Efficacy of a structured, systematic language curriculum for adolescent poor readers. *Reading & Writing Quarterly, 20*(2), 145–159.

Møller, H. L., Mortensen, J. O., & Elbro, C. (2021). Effects of integrated spelling in phonics instruction for at-risk children in kindergarten. *Reading & Writing Quarterly*, 1–16.

Morgan, P. L., Sideridis, G., & Hua, Y. (2012). Initial and over-time effects of fluency interventions for students with or at risk for disabilities. *The Journal of Special Education, 46*(2), 94–116.

Murphy Odo, D. (2024). The use of decodable texts in the teaching of reading in children without reading disabilities: A meta-analysis. *Literacy, 58*(3), 267–277.

Musti-Rao, S., Hawkins, R. O., & Barkley, E. A. (2009). Effects of repeated readings on the oral reading fluency of urban fourth-grade students: Implications for practice. *Preventing School Failure: Alternative Education for Children and Youth, 54*(1), 12–23.

Nagy, W. E., & Scott, J. A. (2000). Vocabulary processes. In M. L. Kamil, P. B. Mosenthal, P. D. Pearson, & R. Barr (Eds.), *Handbook of reading research* (*Vol. 3*, pp. 269–284). Lawrence Erlbaum.

Nash, H., & Snowling, M. (2006). Teaching new words to children with poor existing vocabulary knowledge: A controlled evaluation of the definition and context methods. *International Journal of Language & Communication Disorders, 41*(3), 335–354.

Nation, K., Angell, P., & Castles, A. (2007). Orthographic learning via self-teaching in children learning to read English: Effects of exposure, durability, and context. *Journal of Experimental Child Psychology, 96*(1), 71–84.

Nation, P. (2014). How much input do you need to learn the most frequent 9,000 words? *Reading in a Foreign Language, 26*(2), 1–16.

National Reading Panel (2000). *Report of the National Reading Panel: Teaching children to read: An evidence-based assessment of the scientific research literature on reading and its implications for reading instruction: Reports*.

Ng, Melvin M. R., Bowers, P. N., & Bowers, J. S. (2022). A promising new tool for literacy instruction: The morphological matrix. *PLOS One, 17*(1).

Nielsen, A. M. V., Daugaard, H. T., Scavenius, C., & Juul, H. (2022). Combining morphological and contextual strategy instruction to enhance word learning. *International Journal of Educational Research, 112*, 101920.

Nielsen, D. C., & Friesen, L. D. (2012). A study of the effectiveness of a small-group intervention on the vocabulary and narrative development of at-risk kindergarten children. *Reading Psychology, 33*(3), 269–299.

Nielsen, J. L., Christensen, R. V., & Poulsen, M. (2025). Syntactic comprehension—A separate source of individual variance in middle-school children's reading comprehension. *Reading Research Quarterly, 60*(2), e70003.

Nilsson, N. L. (2008). A critical analysis of eight informal reading inventories. *The Reading Teacher, 61*(7), 526–536.

Novelli, C., Ardoin, S. P., & Rodgers, D. B. (2024). Seeing the mouth: The importance of articulatory gestures during phonics training. *Reading and Writing, 37*(10), 2521–2547.

O'Connor, R. E., Beach, K. D., Sanchez, V. M., Bocian, K. M., & Flynn, L. J. (2015). Building BRIDGES: A design experiment to improve reading and United States history knowledge of poor readers in eighth grade. *Exceptional Children, 81*, 399–425.

Oakes, W. P., Lane, K. L., Menzies, H. M., & Buckman, M. M. (2018). Instructional feedback: An effective, efficient, low-intensity strategy to support student success. *Beyond Behavior, 27*(3), 168–174.

Parker, D. C., Zaslofsky, A. F., Burns, M. K., Kanive, R., Hodgson, J., Scholin, S. E., & Klingbeil, D. A. (2015). A brief report of the diagnostic accuracy of oral reading fluency and reading inventory levels for reading failure risk among second- and third-grade students. *Reading & Writing Quarterly, 31*(1), 56–67.

Peng, P., Wang, W., Filderman, M. J., Zhang, W., & Lin, L. (2024). The active ingredient in reading comprehension strategy intervention for struggling readers: A Bayesian network meta-analysis. *Review of Educational Research, 94*(2), 228–267.

Perfetti, C., & Stafura, J. (2014). Word knowledge in a theory of reading comprehension. *Scientific Studies of Reading, 18*(1), 22–37.

Petersen, D. B., Chanthongthip, H., Ukrainetz, T. A., Spencer, T. D., & Steeve, R. W. (2017). Dynamic assessment of narratives: Efficient, accurate identification of language impairment in bilingual students. *Journal of Speech, Language, and Hearing Research, 60*(4), 983–998.

Piasta, S. B., Hudson, A. K., Logan, J. A., Lewis, K., & Zettler-Greeley, C. M. (2025). Alphabet knowledge trajectories and U.S. children's later reading and spelling. *Scientific Studies of Reading, 29*(3), 303–327.

Pikulski, J. (1974). A critical review: Informal reading inventories. *The Reading Teacher, 28*(2), 141–151.

Pitcher, B., & Fang, Z. (2007). Can we trust leveled texts? An examination of their reliability and quality from a linguistic perspective. *Literacy, 41*(1), 43–51.

Poulsen, M., & Gravgaard, A. K. (2016). Who did what to whom? The relationship between syntactic aspects of sentence comprehension and text comprehension. *Scientific Studies of Reading, 20*(4), 325–338.

Priebe, S. J., Keenan, J. M., & Miller, A. C. (2012). How prior knowledge affects word identification and comprehension. *Reading and Writing, 25*(1), 131–149.

Pritchard, V. E., Malone, S. A., & Hulme, C. (2021). Early handwriting ability predicts the growth of children's spelling, but not reading, skills. *Scientific Studies of Reading, 25*(4), 304–318.

Proctor, C. P., Silverman, R. D., Harring, J. R., Jones, R. L., & Hartranft, A. M. (2020). Teaching bilingual learners: Effects of a language-based reading intervention on academic language and reading comprehension in grades 4 and 5. *Reading Research Quarterly, 55*(1), 95–122.

Pullen, P. C., & Lane, H. B. (2016). Hands-on decoding: Guidelines for using manipulative letters. *Learning Disabilities: A Multidisciplinary Journal, 21*(1), 27–37.

Puzio, K., Colby, G. T., & Algeo-Nichols, D. (2020). Differentiated literacy instruction: Boondoggle or best practice? *Review of Educational Research, 90*(4), 459–498.

Pyle, N., Vasquez, A. C., Lignugaris/Kraft, B., Gillam, S. L., Reutzel, D. R., Olszewski, A., & Pyle, D. (2017). Effects of expository text structure interventions on comprehension: A meta-analysis. *Reading Research Quarterly, 52*(4), 469–501.

Rapp, D. N., Broek, P. V. D., McMaster, K. L., Kendeou, P., & Espin, C. A. (2007). Higher-order comprehension processes in struggling readers: A perspective for research and intervention. *Scientific Studies of Reading, 11*(4), 289–312.

Rasinski, T. V. (1990). The effects of cued phrase boundaries on reading performance: A review.

Rasinski, T. V. (2004). Assessing reading fluency. Pacific Resources for Education and Learning (PREL).

Rasinski, T. V., & Smith, M. C. (2025). *The megabook of fluency* (2nd ed.). Scholastic.

Rasinski, T., Samuels, S. J., Hiebert, E., Petscher, Y., & Feller, K. (2011). The relationship between a silent reading fluency instructional protocol on students' reading comprehension and achievement in an urban school setting. *Reading Psychology, 32*(1), 75–97.

Ray, K., Dally, K., Rowlandson, L., Tam, K. I., & Lane, A. E. (2022). The relationship of handwriting ability and literacy in kindergarten: A systematic review. *Reading and Writing, 35*(5), 1119–1155.

Rehfeld, D. M., Kirkpatrick, M., O'Guinn, N., & Renbarger, R. (2022). A meta-analysis of phonemic awareness instruction provided to children suspected of having a reading disability. *Language, Speech, and Hearing Services in Schools, 53*(4), 1177–1201.

Reis, S. M., McCoach, D. B., Little, C. A., Muller, L. M., & Kaniskan, R. B. (2011). The effects of differentiated instruction and enrichment pedagogy on reading achievement in five elementary schools. *American Educational Research Journal, 48*(2), 462–501.

Rice, M., & Wijekumar, K. K. (2024). Inference skills for reading: A meta-analysis of instructional practices. *Journal of Educational Psychology, 116*(4), 569.

Rice, M., Erbeli, F., & Wijekumar, K. (2024). Phonemic awareness: Evidence-based instruction for students in need of intervention. *Intervention in School and Clinic, 59*(4), 269–273.

Rice, M., Erbeli, F., Thompson, C. G., Sallese, M. R., & Fogarty, M. (2022). Phonemic awareness: A meta-analysis for planning effective instruction. *Reading Research Quarterly, 57*(4), 1259–1289.

Roberts, G. J., Hall, C., Cho, E., Coté, B., Lee, J., Qi, B., & Van Ooyik, J. (2022). The state of current reading intervention research for English learners in grades K–2: A best-evidence synthesis. *Educational Psychology Review, 34*(1), 335–361.

Roberts, T. A. (2005). Articulation accuracy and vocabulary size contributions to phonemic awareness and word reading in English Language learners. *Journal of Educational Psychology, 97*(4), 601.

Roberts, T. A. (2021). Learning letters: Evidence and questions from a science-of-reading perspective. *Reading Research Quarterly, 56*, S171–S192.

Roberts, T. A., & Sadler, C. D. (2019). Letter sound characters and imaginary narratives: Can they enhance motivation and letter sound learning? *Early Childhood Research Quarterly, 46*, 97–111.

Roberts, T. A., Vadasy, P. F., & Sanders, E. A. (2019). Preschoolers' alphabet learning: Cognitive, teaching sequence, and English proficiency influences. *Reading Research Quarterly, 54*(3), 413–437.

Rodgers, E., D'Agostino, J. V., Harmey, S. J., Kelly, R. H., & Brownfield, K. (2016). Examining the nature of scaffolding in an early literacy intervention. *Reading Research Quarterly, 51*(3), 345–360.

Rodgers, E., D'Agostino, J. V., Levin, J. R., & Rasinski, T. (2025). Pairing phrase-cued text with readers theatre: Effects on reading prosody and automaticity. *Journal of Research in Reading, 48*(2), 153–174.

Ross, K. M., & Joseph, L. M. (2019). Effects of word boxes on improving students' basic literacy skills: A literature review. *Preventing School Failure: Alternative Education for Children & Youth, 63*(1), 43–51.

Saddler, B. (2012). *Teacher's guide to effective sentence writing*. Guilford Press.

Saddler, B., Ellis-Robinson, T., & Asaro-Saddler, K. (2018). Using sentence combining instruction to enhance the writing skills of children with learning disabilities. *Learning Disabilities: A Contemporary Journal, 16*(2), 191–202.

Santangelo, T., & Graham, S. (2016). A comprehensive meta-analysis of handwriting instruction. *Educational Psychology Review, 28*(2), 225–265.

Sargiani, R. D. A., Ehri, L. C., & Maluf, M. R. (2022). Teaching beginners to decode consonant-vowel syllables using grapheme-phoneme subunits facilitates reading and spelling as compared with teaching whole-syllable decoding. *Reading Research Quarterly, 57*(2), 629–648.

Savage, R., Georgiou, G. K., Inoue, T., Dunn, K., & Parrila, R. (2025). Set-for-variability predicts responsiveness to tier 2 reading interventions. *Scientific Studies of Reading, 29*(2), 115–137.

Savage, R., Georgiou, G., Parrila, R., & Maiorino, K. (2018). Preventative reading interventions teaching direct mapping of graphemes in texts and set-for-variability aid at-risk learners. *Scientific Studies of Reading, 22*(3), 225–247.

Scarborough, H. S. (2001). Connecting early language and literacy to later reading (dis)abilities: Evidence, theory, and practice. In S. B. Neuman & D. K. Dickinson (Eds.), *Handbook of early literacy research* (Vol. 1, pp. 97–110). Guilford Press.

Scammacca, N. K., Roberts, G., Vaughn, S., & Stuebing, K. K. (2015). A meta-analysis of interventions for struggling readers in grades 4–12: 1980–2011. *Journal of Learning Disabilities, 48*(4), 369–390.

Schall, M., Skinner, C. H., Cazzell, S., Ciancio, D., Ruddy, J., & Thompson, K. (2016). Extending research on oral reading fluency measures, reading speed, and comprehension. *Contemporary School Psychology, 20*(3), 262–269.

Seabrook, R., Brown, G. D., & Solity, J. E. (2005). Distributed and massed practice: From laboratory to classroom. *Applied Cognitive Psychology, 19*(1), 107–122.

Share, D. L. (2004). Orthographic learning at a glance: On the time course and developmental onset of self-teaching. *Journal of Experimental Child Psychology, 87*(4), 267–298.

Sharp, L., & Brown, T. (2015). Handwriting instruction: An analysis of perspectives from three elementary teachers. *Texas Journal of Literacy Education, 3*(1), 29–37.

Shefelbine, J., & Calhoun, J. (1991). Variability in approaches to identifying polysyllabic words: A descriptive study of sixth graders with highly, moderately, and poorly developed syllabification strategies. *Learner Factors/Teacher Factors: Issues in Literacy Research and Instruction*, 169–177.

Shhub, A., Jimenez, Z., & Solis, M. (2023). A synthesis of reading prosody: Evaluating phrasing and syntax interventions. *Reading & Writing Quarterly, 39*(6), 530–547.

Siegal, S. W., Hall, C., & Mesa, M. P. (2024). *Aligning practice with research: Using small groups to differentiate instruction.* Topic Paper. Scholastic.

Silverman, R. D., Johnson, E., Keane, K., & Khanna, S. (2020). Beyond decoding: A meta-analysis of the effects of language comprehension interventions on K–5 students' language and literacy outcomes. *Reading Research Quarterly, 55*, S207–S233.

Slavin, R. E. (1993). Ability grouping in the middle grades: Achievement effects and alternatives. *The Elementary School Journal, 93*(5), 535–552.

Slavin, R. E., Lake, C., Davis, S., & Madden, N. A. (2011). Effective programs for struggling readers: A best-evidence synthesis. *Educational Research Review, 6*(1), 1–26.

Smith, R., Snow, P., Serry, T., & Hammond, L. (2021). The role of background knowledge in reading comprehension: A critical review. *Reading Psychology, 42*(3), 214–240.

Spector, J. E. (2005). How reliable are informal reading inventories? *Psychology in the Schools, 42*(6), 593–603.

Stalega, M. V., Kearns, D. M., Bourget, J., Bayer, N., & Hebert, M. (2024). Is phonological-only instruction helpful for reading? A meta-analysis. *Scientific Studies of Reading, 28*(6), 614–635.

Steacy, L. M., Wade-Woolley, L., Rueckl, J. G., Pugh, K. R., Elliott, J. D., & Compton, D. L. (2019). The role of set for variability in irregular word reading: Word and child predictors in typically developing readers and students at-risk for reading disabilities. *Scientific Studies of Reading, 23*(6), 523–532.

Steenbergen-Hu, S., Makel, M. C., & Olszewski-Kubilius, P. (2016). What one hundred years of research says about the effects of ability grouping and acceleration on K–12 students' academic achievement: Findings of two second-order meta-analyses. *Review of Educational Research, 86*(4), 849–899.

Stevens, E. A., & Vaughn, S. (2021). Using paraphrasing and text structure instruction to support main idea generation. *Teaching Exceptional Children, 53*(4), 300–308.

Stevens, E. A., Vaughn, S., Swanson, E., & Scammacca, N. (2020). Examining the effects of a tier 2 reading comprehension intervention aligned to tier 1 instruction for fourth-grade struggling readers. *Exceptional Children, 86*(4), 430–448.

Stevens, E. A., Walker, M. A., & Vaughn, S. (2017). The effects of reading fluency interventions on the reading fluency and reading comprehension performance of elementary students with learning disabilities: A synthesis of the research from 2001 to 2014. *Journal of Learning Disabilities, 50*(5), 576–590.

Strong, J. Z. (2020). Investigating a text structure intervention for reading and writing in grades 4 and 5. *Reading Research Quarterly, 55*(4), 545–551.

Strong, J. Z., Amendum, S. J., & Conradi Smith, K. (2018). Supporting elementary students' reading of difficult texts. *The Reading Teacher, 72*(2), 201–212.

Suggate, S. P. (2016). A meta-analysis of the long-term effects of phonemic awareness, phonics, fluency, and reading comprehension interventions. *Journal of Learning Disabilities, 49*(1), 77–96.

Teng, F. (2016). The effects of word exposure frequency on incidental learning of the depth of vocabulary knowledge. *GEMA Online® Journal of Language Studies, 16*(3), 53–70.

Therrien, W. J. (2004). Fluency and comprehension gains as a result of repeated reading: A meta-analysis. *Remedial and Special Education, 25*(4), 252–261.

Torgesen, J. K., & Hudson, R. F. (2006). Reading fluency: Critical issues for struggling readers. In S. J. Samuels & A. E. Farstrup (Eds.), *What research has to say about fluency instruction* (pp. 130–158). International Reading Association.

Torppa, M., Poikkeus, A. M., Laakso, M. L., Eklund, K., & Lyytinen, H. (2006). Predicting delayed letter name knowledge and its relation to grade 1 reading achievement in children with and without familial risk for dyslexia. *Developmental Psychology*, (6).

Tortorelli, L. S., & Truckenmiller, A. J. (2024). Automaticity in writing in response to reading: relations between oral reading fluency and compositional writing fluency in grades 3–5. *Reading & Writing Quarterly, 40*(2), 103–117.

Tortorelli, L. S., Strong, J. Z., & Anderson, B. E. (2024). Multisyllabic decoding achievement and relation to vocabulary at the end of elementary school. *Journal of Experimental Child Psychology, 246*, 106018.

Toste, J. R., Fluhler, S. K., Farris, E. A., & Chandler, B. W. (2025). What's in a word? Analyzing students' oral reading fluency to inform instructional decision-making. *Intervention in School and Clinic, 60*(5), 251–261.

Toste, J. R., Williams, K. J., & Capin, P. (2017). Reading big words: Instructional practices to promote multisyllabic word reading fluency. *Intervention in School and Clinic, 52*(5), 270–278.

Truckenmiller, A., Coyne, M., Valentine, K., Moura, P., & Sarmiento, C. (2025). Independent researcher review of commercial reading screening assessment suites, May 2025.

Tunmer, W. E., & Chapman, J. W. (2012). The simple view of reading redux: Vocabulary knowledge and the independent components hypothesis. *Journal of Learning Disabilities, 45*(5), 453–466.

Uribe, S. N. (2019). Curriculum-based readers theatre as an approach to literacy and content area instruction for English language learners. *Reading & Writing Quarterly, 35*(3), 243–260.

Vadasy, P. F., Sanders, E. A., & Nelson, J. R. (2015). Effectiveness of supplemental kindergarten vocabulary instruction for English learners: A randomized study of immediate and longer-term effects of two approaches. *Journal of Research on Educational Effectiveness, 8*(4), 490–529.

Vadasy, P. F., Sanders, E. A., & Peyton, J. A. (2006). Paraeducator-supplemented instruction in structural analysis with text reading practice for second and third graders at risk for reading problems. *Remedial and Special Education, 27*(6), 365–378.

van Bergen, E., Vasalampi, K., & Torppa, M. (2021). How are practice and performance related? Development of reading from ages 5 to 15. *Reading Research Quarterly, 56*(3), 415–434.

van Rijthoven, R., Kleemans, T., Segers, E., & Verhoeven, L. (2021). Response to phonics through spelling intervention in children with dyslexia. *Reading & Writing Quarterly, 37*(1), 17–31.

Verhoeven, L., Voeten, M., van Setten, E., & Segers, E. (2020). Computer-supported early literacy intervention effects in preschool and kindergarten: A meta-analysis. *Educational Research Review, 30*, 100325.

Walpole, S., & McKenna, M. C. (2017). *How to plan differentiated reading instruction: Resources for grades K–3.* Guilford Press.

Wang, Z., Sabatini, J., O'Reilly, T., & Weeks, J. (2019). Decoding and reading comprehension: A test of the decoding threshold hypothesis. *Journal of Educational Psychology, 111*(3), 387.

Wanzek, J., Stevens, E. A., Williams, K. J., Scammacca, N., Vaughn, S., & Sargent, K. (2018). Current evidence on the effects of intensive early reading interventions. *Journal of Learning Disabilities, 51*(6), 612–624.

Wanzek, J., Vaughn, S., Scammacca, N., Gatlin, B., Walker, M. A., & Capin, P. (2016). Meta-analyses of the effects of tier 2 type reading interventions in grades K–3. *Educational Psychology Review, 28*(3), 551–576.

Weiser, B., & Mathes, P. (2011). Using encoding instruction to improve the reading and spelling performances of elementary students at risk for literacy difficulties: A best-evidence synthesis. *Review of Educational Research, 81*(2), 170–200.

Wijekumar, K. K., Hudson, A., Lambright, K., Owens, J. K., Binks-Cantrell, E., Beerwinkle, A., & Stack, A. (2023). Knowledge acquisition and transformation (KAT) using text structures. *The Reading League Journal*, 33–39.

Williams, J. P. (2018). Text structure instruction: The research is moving forward. *Reading and Writing, 31*(9), 1923–1935.

Wise, C. N., & Duke, N. K. (2025). Assessment of skill in inferring unfamiliar word meanings. *Reading and Writing*, 1–29.

Wisniewski, B., Zierer, K., & Hattie, J. (2020). The power of feedback revisited: A meta-analysis of educational feedback research. *Frontiers in Psychology, 10*, 487662.

Wolters, A. P., Kim, Y. S. G., & Szura, J. W. (2022). Is reading prosody related to reading comprehension? A meta-analysis. *Scientific Studies of Reading, 26*(1), 1–20.

Wyatt, T., & Chapman-DeSousa, B. (2017). Teaching as interaction: Challenges in transitioning teachers' instruction to small groups. *Early Childhood Education Journal, 45*, 61–70.

Young, C., & Rasinski, T. (2009). Implementing readers theatre as an approach to classroom fluency instruction. *The Reading Teacher, 63*(1), 4–13.

Young, C., Durham, P., Miller, M., Rasinski, T. V., & Lane, F. (2019). Improving reading comprehension with readers theater. *The Journal of Educational Research, 112*(5), 615–626.

Young, C., Durham, P., Rasinski, T. V., Godwin, A., & Miller, M. (2021). Closing the gender gap in reading with readers theater. *The Journal of Educational Research, 114*(5), 495–511.

Zipoli Jr., R. P. (2017). Unraveling difficult sentences: Strategies to support reading comprehension. *Intervention in School and Clinic, 52*(4), 218–227.

Index